Full Stack JavaScript

Learn Backbone.js, Node.js, and MongoDB

Second Edition

Azat Mardan

Apress®

Full Stack JavaScript: Learn Backbone.js, Node.js, and MongoDB

Azat Mardan
San Francisco, California, USA

ISBN-13 (pbk): 978-1-4842-3717-5   ISBN-13 (electronic): 978-1-4842-3718-2
https://doi.org/10.1007/978-1-4842-3718-2

Library of Congress Control Number: 2018962263

Managing Director, Apress Media LLC: Welmoed Spahr
Acquisitions Editor: Louise Corrigan
Development Editor: James Markham
Coordinating Editor: Nancy Chen

Cover designed by eStudioCalamar

Distributed to the book trade worldwide by Springer Science+Business Media New York, 233 Spring Street, 6th Floor, New York, NY 10013. Phone 1-800-SPRINGER, fax (201) 348-4505, e-mail orders-ny@springer-sbm.com, or visit www.springeronline.com. Apress Media, LLC is a California LLC and the sole member (owner) is Springer Science + Business Media Finance Inc (SSBM Finance Inc). SSBM Finance Inc is a **Delaware** corporation.

For information on translations, please e-mail rights@apress.com, or visit http://www.apress.com/rights-permissions.

Apress titles may be purchased in bulk for academic, corporate, or promotional use. eBook versions and licenses are also available for most titles. For more information, reference our Print and eBook Bulk Sales web page at http://www.apress.com/bulk-sales.

Any source code or other supplementary material referenced by the author in this book is available to readers on GitHub via the book's product page, located at www.apress.com/9781484237175. For more detailed information, please visit http://www.apress.com/source-code.

Printed on acid-free paper

To my parents, Almas and Alsu, who bought me my first computer, and let me use the phone line for dial-up Internet.

Table of Contents

About the Author

Azat Mardan has over 18 years of experience in web, mobile, and software development. With a Bachelor's degree in Informatics and a Master of Science degree in Information Systems Technology, Azat possesses deep academic knowledge as well as extensive practical experience. Azat is an experienced software engineer, author, and educator. He has published 16 books and counting.

Currently, Azat works as a Software Engineering Leader at Indeed.com, the number one job search site. Before Azat worked as a Technology Fellow at Capital One Financial Corporation, a top 10 USA bank. Even before that, Azat was a Team Lead at DocuSign, where his team rebuilt 50 million user products (DocuSign web app) using the tech stack of Node.js, Express.js, Backbone.js, CoffeeScript, Jade, Stylus, and Redis.

Recently, he worked as a senior engineer at the curated social media news aggregator web site, `Storify.com` (now part of Adobe), which is used by BBC, NBC, CNN, the White House, and others. Storify runs everything on Node.js unlike other companies. It's the maintainer of the open source library jade browser.

Before that, Azat worked as a CTO/Cofounder at Gizmo—an enterprise cloud platform for mobile marketing campaigns, and has undertaken the prestigious 500 Startups business accelerator program.

Azat also has past experience developing mission-critical applications for government agencies in Washington, DC, including the National Institutes of Health, the National Center for Biotechnology Information, and the Federal Deposit Insurance Corporation, as well as for Lockheed Martin.

Azat is a frequent attendee at Bay Area tech meet-ups and hackathons (AngelHack hackathon '12 finalist with team `FashionMetric.com`, which went on to raise venture capital from Mark Cuban and TechStars).

In addition, Azat teaches technical classes at General Assembly, Hack Reactor, pariSOMA, and Marakana (acquired by Twitter) to much acclaim.

In his spare time, he writes about technology on his blog: `Webapplog.com`, which was a number one in "express.js tutorial" Google search results for some time.

Azat is also the author of *Pro Express.js, Practical Node.js, Node Program* (`http://nodeprogram.com/`) and others. Azat is the creator of open source Node.js projects, including ExpressWorks, mongoui, and HackHall.

You can reach Azat and say hi using one of these methods:

Twitter: @azatmardan `https://twitter.com/azatmardan` - Azat loves getting "Hi" on Twitter

LinkedIn: `linkedin.com/in/azatm`

Blog: `webapplog.com`

GitHub: `github.com/azat-co/fullstack-javascript`

Acknowledgments

I would like to thank the team of early Node contributors bringing JavaScript to the servers. Without them, the full stack JavaScript development wouldn't be possible.

Thank you to the supporters of my Kickstarter campaign to write the second edition of this book and do so in the open on GitHub. Without you I probably would have not worked on this release so hard and maybe not worked at all. You are AWESOME because you made this new edition a reality and not only that but you have made this edition and previous edition available on GitHub for the entire world to read and learn Node which is the greatest technology for building web applications ever.

In particular, very great many thanks to individual Kickstarter supporters (who will soon get the signed print books and other rewards or maybe already have them): Matthew Amacker, Jordan Horiuchi, Tim Chen, Alexey Bushnev, Aleksey Maksimov, Maurice van Cooten, Ryan, Ng Yao Min, Kommana Karteek, Elias Yousef, Arhuman, Javier Armendariz, Dave Anderson, Edithson Abelard. You guys are brilliant!

I cannot not mention the biggest supporter DevelopIntelligence, which is one of the best if not the best tech training companies in the world (http://www.developintelligence.com). So if you need to train your software engineers in... anything! Then email them. Seriously, Develop Intelligence has been around for 10+ years, and they have great teachers with great technical classes. I was one of their instructors so I know. :)

I'm grateful to my copy and content editors at Apress, specifically to James Markham, Louise Corrigan, Teresa Horton, and Karen Jameson. They accomplished an amazing feat by bringing this book to life in a span of a few weeks.

ACKNOWLEDGMENTS

Also, I'm grateful to the students of Hack Reactor, Marakana, pariSOMA, and General Assembly where I taught and used early Full Stack JavaScript (or its parts) training material.

Once again, big thanks goes to Develop Intelligence who backed my effort to open source the manuscript of this book and allowed me to work in the open with early readers. I taught many corporate workshop on React, Node, cloud, and JavaScript to clients of Develop Intelligence. If you wants a world-class on-site tech training, go to developintelligence.com and book the class.

Preface

I'm writing this as I'm sitting at the San Francisco airport waiting for my flight to Portland, Oregon, for the biggest Node.js conference. I'll be speaking there about Node.js. It's scary and funny at the same time to think that I started to learn Node only three years ago. Yes, I remember how I decided that the best way to learn is to teach others. For this reason I started teaching my first Node classes and writing this book. The book was mostly for me, so I could remember how to push Heroku or how to create Node servers that talk to MongoDB. It was called *Rapid Prototyping with JS* back then. Three years sped away; I published a few more Node books as well as released several Node apps in production; and in 2014, Apress approached me wanting to publish an updated edition under a new title. I can't believe this is the second editon of the book. It's 2018 and a lot of thing changes. I am glad for the evolution of JavaScript and innovation in the Node.js space.

The main reason I bet my time and energy on JavaScript and Node in the first place is that I felt both intuitively and logically the potential of the full stack JavaScript. The one language to rule the whole stack across all the layers. Logically I understood the code reuse, expressiveness, and performance advantages of Node.js and the ever-increasing importance of front-end development with MVC-like frameworks such as Backbone. Intuitively, I just freaking fell in love with JavaScript both on the browser and on the server.

Yes, I used JavaScript for many years but it was more pain than fun. Not anymore. I was able to get a sense of what's going on at the front end while at the same time getting all the power and flexibility on the server. My brain started to think 5, maybe 10 times faster than before because I started to remember all the obscure methods from Array or String objects. I stopped having Mozilla Developer Network or Google open next to my code editor. And what a relief when you don't need to wait for the compiler each time that you want to test something really quickly.

The airline crew announced my boarding. I need to get on the plane, but I hope this easy, beginner-friendly manual will open the world of full stack JavaScript and cloud computing. Jump on board this amazing technology with me.

Introduction

The kind of programming that C provides will probably remain similar absolutely or slowly decline in usage, but relatively, JavaScript or its variants, or XML, will continue to become more central.

— Dennis Ritchie

In this introduction, we cover:

- Reasons behind full stack JavaScript development in general and for the writing of this book

- What to expect and what not to expect, and what are the prerequisites

- Suggestions on how to use the book and examples

- Explanation of the book's notation format

Full Stack JavaScript is a hands-on book that introduces you to rapid software prototyping using the latest cutting-edge web and mobile technologies including Node.js, MongoDB, Twitter Bootstrap, LESS, jQuery, Parse.com, Heroku, and others.

Why This Book?

This book was borne out of frustration. I have been in software engineering for many years, and when I started learning Node.js and Backbone.js, I learned the hard way that their official documentation and the Internet lack good quick start guides and examples. Needless to say, it was virtually impossible to find all of the tutorials for JS-related modern technologies in one place.

The best way to learn is to do, right? Therefore, I used the approach of small, simple examples (that is, quick start guides) to expose myself to the new cool tech. After I was done with the basic apps, I needed some references and organization. I started to write this manual mostly for myself, so I could understand the concepts better and refer to the samples later. Then StartupMonthly and I taught a few two-day intensive classes on the same subject—helping experienced developers to jump-start their careers with only-one-language development, that is, JavaScript. The manual we used was updated and iterated many times based on the feedback received. The end result is this book.

Why Go Full Stack JavaScript?

The reasons I love developing with full stack JavaScript, or as others call it universal or isomorphic JavaScript, are numerous:

- *Code reuse*: I can share my libraries, templates, and models between the browser and the server.

- *No context switch*: My brain learns and thinks faster, leaving me more time to work on the actual tasks at hand.

- *Great ecosystem*: npm!

- *Vibrant community*: They are approachable and eager to help.

- *Great masters*: A treasure chest of knowledge and best practices has accumulated through the years of browser JavaScript.

- *Tons of tutorials and good books*: JavaScript is the most popular language, hence more people are writing about it.

- *No compilation*: Development is faster with interpreted platforms.

- *Good performance*: Node's non-blocking I/O is fast.

- *Evolving standard*: EMCA is constantly pushing new and better versions of JavaScript.

I'm sure I've missed a few points, but you got the idea. Whatever the drawbacks of ES5 (the language most of us know as JavaScript) are, they were fixed in ES6/ES2015 and newer versions. The future for JavaScript is so bright we all will have to code with sunglasses on.

What to Expect

Full Stack JavaScript readers should expect a collection of quick start guides, tutorials, and suggestions (for example, Git workflow). There is a lot of coding and not much theory. All the theory we cover is directly related to some of the practical aspects and is essential for better understanding of technologies and specific approaches to dealing with them (for example, JSONP and cross-domain calls).

In addition to coding examples, the book covers virtually all setup and deployment step by step.

You'll learn on the examples of the Message Board application starting with front-end components. There are a few versions of these applications, but by the end of the book we'll put the front end and back end together and deploy to the production environment. The Message Board application contains all of the necessary components typical for a basic web app, and building it will give you enough confidence to continue developing on your own, apply for a job/promotion, or build a startup!

Who This Book Is For

The book is designed for advanced-beginner and intermediate-level web and mobile developers: somebody who has been (or still is) an expert in other languages like Ruby on Rails, PHP, Perl, Python, or/and Java. He/she is the type of developer, who quickly wants to learn more about JavaScript and Node.js-related techniques for building web and mobile application prototypes. The target reader doesn't have time to dig through voluminous (or tiny, at the other extreme) official documentation. The goal of *Full Stack JavaScript* is not to make an expert out of a reader, but to help him/her to start building apps as soon as possible.

As the full title indicates, *Full Stack JavaScript: Learn Backbone.js, Node.js and MongoDB* is about turning your idea into a functional prototype in the form of a web or mobile application as fast as possible. This approach adheres to the Lean Startup methodology; therefore, this book would be more valuable to startup founders, but big companies' employees will also find it useful, especially if they plan to add new skills to their resumes.

What This Book Is Not

Full Stack JavaScript is neither a comprehensive book on several frameworks, libraries, or technologies (or just a particular one), nor a reference for all the tips and tricks of web development. Examples similar to ones in this book might be publicly available online.

More importantly, if you're not familiar with fundamental programming concepts like loops, if/else statements, arrays, hashes, objects, and functions, you should be aware that you won't find them covered in *Full Stack JavaScript*. Additionally, it would be challenging to follow the examples.

Many volumes of great books have been written on fundamental topics — the list of such resources is at the end of the book in the chapter "Further Reading." The purpose of *Full Stack JavaScript* is to give agile tools without replicating theory of programming and computer science.

Prerequisites

I recommend the following prerequisites to get the full advantage of the examples and materials covered in this book:

- Knowledge of fundamental programming concepts such as objects, functions, data structures (arrays, hashes), loops (for, while), and conditions (if/else, switch)

- Basic web development skills including, but not limited to, HTML and CSS

- Using macOS or UNIX/Linux systems for this book's examples (and for web development in general), although it's still possible to hack your way on a Windows-based system

- Access to the Internet

- 5-20 hours of time

- A credit/debit card, which is required by some cloud services even for free accounts

How to Use the Book

The digital version of this book comes in two formats:

1. PDF: Suited for printing; opens in Adobe Reader, Mac OS X Preview, iOS apps, and other PDF viewers.

2. mobi: Suited for Kindles of all generations as well as desktop and mobile Amazon Kindle apps and Amazon Cloud Reader; to copy to devices use Whispernet or a USB cable, or e-mail it to yourself.

Links to web resources are provided throughout the book. In the e-book version, the table of contents has local hyperlinks that allow you to jump to any part or chapter of the book. This is very useful for referring to certain parts of content later; for example, if you want to look up how to deploy to Heroku, you can quickly jump to the needed commands.

I encourage you to take notes and highlight text as you read it studiously. It will improve your retention of the material.

There is a summary in the beginning of each chapter describing in a few short sentences what examples and topics the particular chapter covers.

Each project comes with a YouTube screencast video. I recommend watching the videos to improve your comprehension. You can watch the videos first or read the text first. The videos are supplemental, so it's not a big deal if you are reading the digital book offline or the print book and don't have the ability to watch the video. The text covers everything in the videos. The reason I recorded the screencasts is because people learn differently; some prefer text and others videos. This way, you can take advantage of both media as well as see certain development steps in action.

For faster navigation between parts, chapters, and sections of the book, please use the book's navigation pane, which is based on the Table of Contents (the screenshot is below).

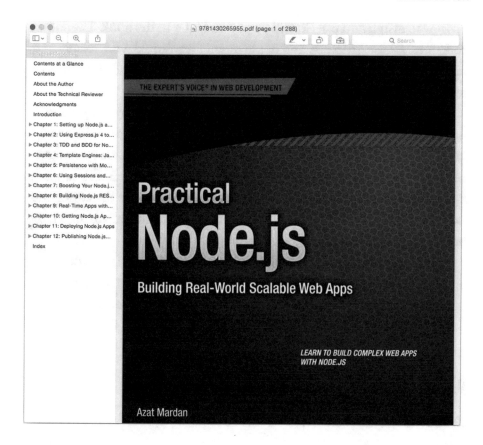

The Table of Contents pane in the Mac OS X Preview app

Examples

All of the source code for examples used in this book is available in the book itself for the most part, as well as at the book's Apress.com product page (`www.apress.com/9781484237175`) and in a public GitHub repository (`https://github.com/azat-co/fullstack-javascript`). You can also download files as a ZIP archive or use Git to pull them. More on how to install and use Git will be covered later in the book. The source code files, folder structure, and deployment files should work locally and/ or remotely on PaaS solutions—that is, Windows Azure and Heroku—with minor or no modifications.

Source code that is in the book is technically limited by the platform to the width of about 70 characters. I tried my best to preserve the best JavaScript and HTML formatting styles, but from time to time you might see backslashes (\). There is nothing wrong with the code. Backslashes are line escape characters, and if you copy-paste the code into the editor, the example should work just fine. Please note that code in GitHub and in the book might differ in formatting.

Last, let me (and others) know if you spot any bugs, by submitting an issue to GitHub! Please, don't send me bug reports in an e-mail, because posting to a public forum like GH Issue will help others, prevent duplicates, and keep everything organized.

Notation

This is what source code blocks look like:

```
var object = {};
object.name = "Bob";
```

Terminal commands have a similar look but start with a dollar sign:

```
$ git push origin heroku
$ cd /etc/
$ ls
```

Inline file names, path/folder names, quotes, and special words/names are italicized, while command names (e.g., mongod and emphasized words, such as Note, are bold.

Terms

For the purposes of this book, we're using some terms interchangeably. Depending on the context, they might not mean exactly the same thing. For example, function = method = call, attribute = property = member = key, value = variable, object = hash = class, list = array, framework = library = module.

Additionally, "full stack" is listed as "fullstack" within code snippets.

PART I

Quick Start

CHAPTER 1

Basics

I think everyone should learn how to program a computer, because it teaches you how to think. I view computer science as a liberal art, something everyone should learn to do.

—Steve Jobs

In this chapter, we'll cover these topics:

- Overview of HTML, CSS, and JavaScript syntaxes

- Brief introduction to Agile methodology

- Advantages of cloud computing, Node.js, and MongoDB

- Descriptions of HTTP requests/responses and RESTful API concepts

In this chapter we will brush up on the fundamental concepts before moving forward. If you are an experienced web developer, then feel free to skip this chapter. If you are new to web development, then pay extra attention. Why? Maybe you have heard and are familiar with some terms, but wonder what they actually mean. Another good reason is that this chapter will cover the RESTful API in a very beginner-friendly manner. REST is used in virtually all modern web architectures, and we'll use it in the book a lot. There is one last reason: You'll look smart at a cocktail party or in front of your colleagues and your boss by acing the hodpodge of web acronyms.

© Azat Mardan 2018
A. Mardan, *Full Stack JavaScript*, https://doi.org/10.1007/978-1-4842-3718-2_1

Front-End Definitions

Front end is a term for browser applications. A browser is called a client because in networking we use client-server communication. Users interact with a client to make requests to a server, which sends back responses. Thus frontend refers to browser or client applications. A client can be a mobile application as well.

Very rarely in some conversations (by some rather old-school Java architects), "front end" is used to define *server* applications. This is very confusing. The only excuse I can make for this usage is that these server apps are facing the browser requests first rather than some other server applications. Or, depending on the context, these server applications act as static web servers to the browser application. To have everything clear and precise, for this book we assume that **when we mention front end it is the browser applications and their code**.

Front-end development, or front-end web development, implies the usage of various technologies. Each of them individually is not too complex, but the sheer number of them makes beginners timid. For example, technologies used include Cascading Style Sheets (CSS), Hypertext Markup Language (HTML), Extensible Markup Language (XML), JavaScript (JS), JavaScript Object Notation (JSON), Uniform Resource Identifier (URI), Hypertext Transfer Protocol (HTTP), Secure Sockets Layer (SSL), Transport Layer Security (TLS), Transmission Control Protocol/Internet Protocol (TCP/IP), Internet Relay Chat (IRC), Remote Procedure Call (RPC), GraphQL, ES, and many other technologies (my next books will be called Swimming in Acronym Soup).

In addition to the low-level technologies, there are numerous frameworks, tools, and libraries; for example, React, jQuery, Backbone.js, Angular.js, Webpack, Grunt, and so on. Please don't confuse front-end frameworks with back-end frameworks: The front-end frameworks run on the browser whereas the back-end ones run on the server.

To build a web application developers have to have multiple things. In a nutshell, front-end web development consists of these components:

1. HTML or templates that compile to HTML

2. Stylesheets to make HTML pretty

3. JavaScript to add interactivity or some business logic to the browser app

4. Some hosting (AWS, Apache, Heroku, etc.)

5. Build scripts to prepare code, manage dependencies, and do pretty much anything that's needed

6. Logic to connect to the server (typically via XHR requests and RESTful API)

Now you know what a job that has the title of front-end developer entails. The great payback to mastering this hodgepodge is the ability to express your creativity by building beautiful and useful apps.

Before we start building, let's cover a bird's-eye view of the web request cycle.

Web Request Cycle

This section is important for someone very new to the web development. The whole World Wide Web or the Internet is about communication between clients and servers. This communication happens by sending requests and receiving responses. Typically browsers (the most popular web clients) send requests to servers. Behind the scenes, servers send their own requests to other servers. Those requests are similar to the browser requests. The language of requests and responses is HTTP(S). Let's explore the browser request in more details.

The browser request consists of the following steps:

1. A user types a URL or follows a link in his or her browser (also called the client).

2. The browser makes an HTTP request to the server.

3. The server processes the request, and if there are any parameters in a query string or body of the request, it takes them into account.

4. The server updates, gets, and transforms data in the database.

5. The server responds with an HTTP response containing data in HTML, JSON, or other formats.

6. The browser receives the HTTP response.

7. The browser renders an HTTP response to the user in HTML or any other format (e.g., JPEG, XML, JSON).

Mobile applications act in the same manner as regular web sites, only instead of a browser there is a native app. Mobile apps (native or HTML5) are just another type of client. Other minor differences between mobile and web include data transfer limitation due to carrier bandwidth, smaller screens, and the more efficient use of local storage. Most likely you, my reader, are a web developer aspiring to use your web chops in mobile. With JavaScript and HTML5 it's possible, so it's worth covering mobile development closer.

Mobile Development

Is mobile going to overtake web and desktop platforms? Maybe, but it's around 2020 and the web traffic is still around 50%. Moreover, the mobile development development field is still somewhat hard and slow compared to the web one. That's good if you are a native mobile developer, but most of us are not. There's a bigger gap in talent compared to web. The gap is closing. With React Native, you can write once in JavaScript and reuse code on iOS and Android. You can build Windows and macOS desktop apps with JavaScript using Electron. There are other approaches to mobile and desktop that leverage JavaScript as well.

These are the approaches to mobile development, each with its own advantages and disadvantages:

1. *Native*: Native iOS, Android, Blackberry apps built Objective-C, Swift, or Java.

2. *Abstracted native*: Native apps built with JavaScript, React Native (`https://facebook.github.io/react-native`), NativeScript, Appcelerator (`https://www.appcelerator.com`), Xamarin, (`https://xamarin.com`), Smartface (`https://www.smartface.io`), or similar tools, and then compiled into native Objective-C or Java.

3. *Responsive*: Mobile websites tailored for smaller screens with responsive design, CSS frameworks like Bootstrap (`https://twitter.github.io/bootstrap`) or Foundation (`https://foundation.zurb.com`), regular CSS, or different templates. You might use some JavaScript frameworks for the development like Backbone.js, Angular.js, Ember.js, or React.js.

4. *Hybrid*: HTML5 apps which consist of HTML, CSS, and JavaScript, and are usually built with frameworks like Sencha Touch (`https://www.sencha.com/products/touch`), Trigger.io (`https://trigger.io`), or Ionic (`https://ionicframework.com`)

and then wrapped into a native app with PhoneGap (`https://phonegap.com`). As in the third approach, you probably will want to use a JavaScript framework for the development such as Backbone.js, Angular.js, Ember.js, or React.js.

My personal favorites are the second and fourth approaches, which are abstracted and hybrid ones. The second approach doesn't require a different code base. A minimal viable product (MVP) can be built across multiple platforms by sharing a lot of the code. I recommend React Native. Check out my book and course *React Native Quickly* (`https://node.university/p/react-native-quickly`) to get started with mobile development using the abstracted approach.

The fourth approach is more powerful and provides more scalable (in a development sense) UIs. This is better suited for complex apps. Code reuse between cross-platform mobile and web is easy because most of the times you're writing in JavaScript.

HyperText Markup Language

HTML is not a real programming language in itself. It is a set of markup tags that describe the content and present it in a structured and formatted way. We cannot code much logic into HTML. There are no variables or loops. HTML is the language of the web because it is ubiquitous and used by all clients (browsers) to interpret the data to users.

HTML tags consist of a tag name inside of the angle brackets (<>). In most cases, tags surround the content, with the end tag having a forward slash before the tag name. Tags create hierarchy of content. Each tag has a meaning, purpose, and a default display representation in a browser. For example, there are tags for headings, paragraphs, bullet points, images, links, and many more items.

In this example, each line is an HTML element:

```html
<h2>Overview of HTML</h2>
<div>HTML is a ...</div>
<link rel="stylesheet" type="text/css" href="style.css" />
```

An HTML document itself is an element of the `<html>` tag, and all other elements such as head, body, h2, and p are children of that `<html>` tag. The tag head is for metadata of the page—info of the page itself, not visible to the user content, while body is for the content (visible to the user). Developers use four-space indentation to signify and mark the nested elements. The element link is two levels nested in the html element. (It includes/imports the CSS style.)

```html
<!DOCTYPE html>
<html lang="en">
    <head>
        <link rel="stylesheet" type="text/css"
        href="style.css"/>
    </head>
    <body>
        <h2>Overview of HTML</h2>
        <p>HTML is a ...</p>
    </body>
</html>
```

Notice that the closing tags have a slash (/) inside the angle brackets (<>), but before the name of the tag, e.g., `</html>`. This is important for proper rendering (interpretation and displaying) of elements by the browser.

There are different flavors and versions of HTML, such as DHTML, XHTML1.0, XHTML1.1, XHTML2, HTML4, and HTML5. This comic strip does a good job of explaining the differences: Misunderstanding Markup: XHTML 2/HTML 5 (https://bit.ly/2N5WTU1). Before HTML5

web developers had to use the appropriate version, but now just write
`<!DOCTYPE html>` and modern browsers will understand your markup.

Any HTML element can have attributes. You already saw `link` with
`rel`, `type`, and `href`. Attributes are typically extra information that is not
directly visible by the user. Attributes are not content and they are different
in this sense from nested elements, which are content. The most important
attributes which are applicable to almost all elements and tags are `class`,
`id`, `style`, and `data-name`. Then there are event attributes such as
`onclick`, `onmouseover`, `onkeyup`, and so on.

class

The `class` attribute defines a class that is used for styling in CSS or
Domain Object Model (DOM) manipulation; for example:

```
<p class="normal">...</p>
```

id

The `id` attribute defines an ID that is similar in purpose to element class,
but it has to be unique; for example:

```
<div id="footer">...</div>
```

style

The `style` attribute defines inline CSS to style an element; for example:

```
<font style="font-size:20px">...</font>
```

title

The `title` attribute specifies additional information that is usually
presented in tooltips by most browsers; for example:

```
<a title="Up-vote the answer">...</a>
```

data-name

The data-name attribute allows for metadata to be stored in the DOM; for example:

```
<tr data-token="fa10a70c-21ca-4e73-aaf5-
d889c7263a0e">...</tr>
```

onclick

The onclick attribute calls inline JavaScript code when a click event happens; for example:

```
<input type="button"
  onclick="validateForm();">...</a>
```

onmouseover

The onmouseover attribute is similar to onclick but for mouse hover events; for example:

```
<a onmouseover="javascript:
  this.setAttribute('css','color:red')">

  ...
</a>
```

Other HTML element attributes for inline JavaScript code are as follows:

- onfocus: When the browser focuses on an element

- onblur: When the browser focus leaves an element

- onkeydown: When a user presses a keyboard key

- ondblclick: When a user double-clicks the mouse

- onmousedown: When a user presses a mouse button

11

- `onmouseup`: When a user releases a mouse button

- `onmouseout`: When a user moves mouse out of the element area

- `oncontextmenu`: When a user opens a context menu

The full list of such events and a browser compatibility table are presented in "Event compatibility tables" (`https://www.quirksmode.org/dom/events/index.html`).

We'll use classes extensively with the Bootstrap framework (`https://getbootstrap.com`), but the use of inline CSS and JavaScript code is generally a bad idea, so we'll try to avoid it. However, it's good to know the names of the JavaScript events because they are used all over the place in jQuery, Backbone.js, and, of course, plain JavaScript. To convert the list of attributes to a list of JS events, just remove the prefix on; for example, `onclick` attribute means click event.

More information is available at MDN: Getting Started with JS (`https://developer.mozilla.org/en-US/docs/JavaScript/Getting_Started`)

Cascading Style Sheets

CSS provides a way to format and present content. An HTML document can have an external stylesheet included in it by a `<link>` tag, as shown in the previous examples, or it can have CSS code directly inside of a `<style>` tag:

```
<style>
  body {
    padding-top: 60px; /* 60px to make some space */
  }
</style>
```

Each HTML element can have `id` attributes, `class` attributes, or both:

```
<div id="main" class="large">
   Lorem ipsum dolor sit amet,
   Duis sit amet neque eu.
</div>
```

In CSS we access elements by their id, class, tag name, and in some edge cases, by parent–child relationships or element attribute value.

This sets the color of all the paragraphs (<p> tag) to gray (#999999 in red-blue-green code):

```
p {
   color: #999999;
}
```

This sets padding of a <div> element with the `id` attribute of main:

```
div#main {
   padding-bottom: 2em;
   padding-top: 3em;
}
```

This sets the font size to 14 pixels for all elements with a `class` attribute large:

```
.large {
   font-size: 14pt;
}
```

This hides <div>, which are direct children of the <body> element:

```
body > div {
   display: none;
}
```

This sets the width to 150 pixels for input for which the `name` attribute is `email`:

```
input[name="email"] {
  width: 150px;
}
```

More information about CSS is available at Wikipedia (`https://en.wikipedia.org/wiki/Cascading_Style_Sheets`) and MDN (`https://developer.mozilla.org/en-US/docs/Web/CSS`).

CSS3 is an upgrade to CSS that includes new ways of doing things such as rounded corners, borders, and gradients, which were possible in regular CSS only with the help of PNG/GIF images and by using other tricks.

For more information refer to CSS3.info (`http://css3.info`), and CSS3 vs. CSS comparison article on Smashing (`http://coding.smashingmagazine.com/2011/04/21/css3-vs-css-a-speed-benchmark`).

JavaScript

JavaScript (JS) was crafted in 1995 at Netscape as LiveScript. Guess what other technology got its start in 1995? Java. It was very hyped and popular, so the LiveScript developers renamed it JavaScript. But Java and JavaScript are very different; they are like ham and hamster. JavaScript has the same relationship with Java as a hamster has with a ham. So please don't confuse one with another. JavaScript is interpreted and run by a JavaScript engine (Google Chrome V8 or Microsoft Chakra or SpiderMonkey) from plain text. Java is compiled to bytecode that is run by the Java Virtual Machine. There are differences in syntax, memory usage, typing, and pretty much anything else.

For most beginner programmers, it's easier to get started with JavaScript than with any other language. JavaScript has a very expressive language and very little setup overhead (just open your browser and start coding). JavaScript is the only native language that runs in the browsers (until we have WebAssembly, but who wants to do that?). This fact alone makes JS the most popular language by the number of runtime environments. Moreover, JavaScript is omnipresent. It can be used almost anywhere!

These days, JavaScript is used for both client-side and server-side web development, as well as in desktop application development, drones, Internet of Things (IoT), and other things. This is the main focus of this book because with JavaScript you can develop across all the layers.

If you are a beginner programmer, then just learn JavaScript and you won't need to learn any other languages. You can use JavaScript for everything like frontend, backend, database, and DevOps, and that will make you a full stack JavaScript developer, my friend!

Let's start with JavaScript in HTML. Putting JS code into a `<script>` tag is the easiest way to use JavaScript in an HTML document:

```html
<script type="text/javascript" language="javascript">
  alert("Hello world!") //simple alert dialog window
</script>
```

Be advised that mixing HTML and JS code is not a good idea, so to separate them we can move the code to an external file, and include it by setting the source attribute `src="filename.js"` on a `<script>` tag; for example, for the `app.js` resource:

```html
<script src="js/app.js" type="text/javascript"
  language="javascript">
</script>
```

Note that the closing `<script/>` tag is mandatory even with an empty element like we have where we include the external source file. In other words, just typing `<script src="js/app.js"...>` will not suffice.

Ways, ways back when dinosaurs roamed the world, browsers knew how to parse and run VBScript (Microsoft Visual Basic script, the same as you use in Excel spreadsheets). Hence, developers were required to specify what the type of script is this: JavaScript, VB, or something else (Java, Flash, and other front-end losers). Luckily, now the modern browsers default to JS because that is the only thing they can run, and because that's the only thing commonly used by developers. Thus, the `type` and `language` attributes over the years became optional in *modern* browsers due to the overwhelming dominance of JavaScript.

Other ways to run JavaScript include the following:

- The inline approach already covered

- WebKit browser Developer Tools and FireBug consoles

- The interactive Node.js shell

One of the advantages of the JavaScript language is that it's loosely typed. This loose or weak typing, as opposed to strong typing (`https://en.wikipedia.org/wiki/Strong_typing`) in languages like C and Java, makes JavaScript a better programming language for prototyping. The following sections introduce some of the main types of JavaScript objects/classes. I wrote "objects/classes" because JavaScript doesn't have classes per se. In JS, objects inherit from objects, which is called prototypal inheritance. Confusing? Wait until you see other types of inheritance, because there are several different ways to implement inheritance.

Going back to types, JavaScript primitive types have wrapper objects/classes that provide extra functionality and static methods. Each primitive has a object/class.

Number Primitives

Number primitives are numerical values; for example:

```
const num = 1
```

The way we define variables is with either `var`, `const` or `let`. `const` and `let` respect scopes created by logical blocks (functions, loops, and conditions), where as `var` does not. The `const` declaration will prevent reassignment. If a developer omits `var`, `const` or `let`, then bad things will happen such as leaking variables to the global scope and name collisions.

The old way was to use `var`. I immediately raise a red flag when I perform a job interview and I see a candidate use `var`. It was responsible for quite a lot of weird bugs, so only developers who are unskilled, not aware of ES2015/ES6 or those who learned JavaScript from w3schools.com would use the `var` statement in our day and age. To learn about 10 main features of ES2015/ES6 that every web developer should know, read this concise but full of examples post: `https://webapplog.com/es6`. For ES7 and ES8 features, I recommend this eloquent blog post from Node University: `https://node.university/blog/1621685/es7es8`.

Number Object

The Number `https://developer.mozilla.org/en-US/docs/JavaScript/Reference/Global_Objects/Number` object and its methods provide added functionality for working with numerical values (int and floats). For example, developers can create a `Number` object with new:

```
const numObj = new Number('123') // Number object
const num = numObj.valueOf() // number primitive
const numStr = numObj.toString() // string representation
console.log(numObj === 123) // false
```

Notice the last line, the number object is not triple equals the number primitive. (=== checks for equality in value and type.) This is because primitive and the object are of different types. Conveniently, JavaScript can automatically convert the types to something similar with double equals (==). Thus, the following code will be print/output true:

```
const numObj = new Number('123') // Number object
console.log(numObj === 123) // false
```

The `Number` method has useful methods such as `parseInt()` that is used to convert values from strings to numbers:

```
17 === "17" // false
17 === Number.parseInt("17", 10) // true
```

String Object

The String object has a lot of useful methods, like `length`, `match()`, and so on; for example, to create a `String` object use `new`:

```
const strObj = new String("abcde") // String object
const str = strObj.valueOf() // string primitive
strObj.match(/ab/)
str.match(/ab/) // both call will work
```

String Primitives

String primitives are sequences of characters inside of single quotes (') or double quotes ("); for example, we can define a string primitive simply by using single quotes:

```
const str = 'React Quickly' // single quotes
const str1 = "React Quickly" // double quotes
console.log(str === str1) // true
const newStr = "abcde".substr(1,2) // newStr is bc
```

In JavaScript, double quotes don't have any special power in addition to defining strings unlike other languages where double quotes signify interpolation. In my opinion, we should get rid of single quotes and just use double quotes because it will remove a lot of arguments about what quotes to use. Typically, developers prefer single quotes because then they can use double quotes inside for HTML attributes values. The downside is that you can't use an apostrophe inside of a single quote string unless you escape it with a backslash (\).

```
'it\'s crazy' // valid string
'it's crazy' // INVALID string
```

For convenience, JavaScript automatically wraps string primitives with String object methods. This is why string primitives have fancy methods like substr too. The triple equals will return false though, because String objects and string primitives are not the same types.

RegExp Object

Regular Expressions or RegExps are patterns of characters used in finding matches, replacing, and testing of strings.

```
const pattern = /[A-Z]+/
'ab'.match(pattern) // null
'AB'.match(pattern) // ["AB"]
```

The match() method returns an array of matches (["AB"]). If all you need is a Boolean true/false, then simply use pattern.test(str). For example:

```
const str = 'A'
const pattern = /[A-Z]+/
pattern.test(str) // true
```

Special Types

When in doubt (when debugging), you can always call `typeof obj`. For example,

```
const obj = {}
console.log(typeof obj) // object
const a = 1
console.log(typeof a) // number
```

Here are some of the special types used in JS:

- `NaN`: Not a number

- `null`: Null, nada, zip

- `undefined`: Undeclared variable

- `function`: Function

JSON

The JSON library allows us to parse and serialize JavaScript objects; for example, we can take a valid JSON string, convert it to a JS object, add a new field c, and then convert the object back into the string `stringObj2` and a pretty string `stringObj3` (with spaces and new lines):

```
const stringObj = '{"a": 1, "b": "hi"}'
const obj = JSON.parse(stringObj)
obj.c = 2
const stringObj2 = JSON.stringify(obj)
console.log(stringObj2) // JSON string {"a":1,"b":"hi",
                                         "c":2}
const stringObj3 = JSON.stringify(obj, null, 2)
// make the string pretty with spaces and new lines
console.log(stringObj2) // prettified JSON string
```

Array Object

Arrays are zero-index-based lists. In JavaScript arrays are objects that have sequential indices as keys. The are two way to create an array: `Array` object and array literal. For example:

```
const arr = new Array() // Array object
const arr = ['apple', 'orange', 'kiwi'] // Array literay
```

Each array inherits all `Array` methods. The Array object has a lot of very useful methods, like `indexOf()`, `map()`, `slice()`, and `join()`. Knowing and using these methods will save you hours of coding and debugging. Make sure that you're familiar with them!

Data Object

I really like JavaScript because it's so easy to create an object. In Java, on the other hand, developers have to define a class, maybe an interface too, then have getters and setters in the class, then instantiate the class into an object. In JavaScript, developers just type `{}` and boom, they got an object! Using curly brackets (`{}`) is called object literal. For example, here's an object with `name`, `url`, and `price` fields:

```
const obj = {
  name: 'Gala',
  url: 'img/gala100x100.jpg',
  price: 129
}
```

or developers can use the `Object` object:

```
const obj = new Object({a: 1})
```

But I don't recommend using the `Object` object. Literal is more eloquent.

`Object` has useful methods such as `Object.keys()`, `Object.entries()` and `Object.values()`.

Objects are passed as reference. It better to clone them with `Object.assign()`, otherwise, modifying the original will modify all the references.

```
const obj1 = {a:1}
const obj2 = obj1 // Reference .
console.log(obj2) // { a: 1 }
obj1.a = 2
console.log(obj2) // Changed { a: 2 }
const obj3 = Object.assign({}, obj1) // Clone
console.log(obj3) // { a: 2 }
obj1.a = 3
console.log(obj3) // Unchanged { a: 2 }
```

Every object inherits from `Object`. Inheritance is done by prototypes, class or function factories. I'll provide more on inheritance patterns later.

Boolean Primitives and Objects

Just as with `String` and `Number`, `Boolean` object supports and an alternative to the primitive boolean. I do not recommend using `Boolean` object, only primitive. Here are the usages:

```
const bool1 = true
const bool2 = false
const boolObj = new Boolean(false)
console.log(bool2 === boolObj) // false
console.log(bool2 == boolObj) // true
```

Date Object

The `Date` objects allow us to work with dates and time; for example:

```
const timestamp = Date.now() // 1368407802561
const d = new Date() //Sun May 12 2013 18:17:11
GMT-0700 (PDT)
```

Math Object

The `Math` object has methods for mathematical constants and functions such as `floor()`, `random()`, `round()`, `sqrt()` and so on; for example:

```
const x = Math.floor(3.4890)
const ran = Math.round(Math.random()*100)
```

Browser Objects

Browser objects give us access to a browser and its properties like URLs; for example:

```
window.location.href = 'http://rapidprototypingwithjs.com'
console.log('test')
```

DOM Objects

DOM objects or DOM nodes are the browser interface to the DOM elements rendered on the page. They have properties such as width, height, position, and so on, and, of course, inner content, which can be another element or text. To get a DOM node, you can use its ID; for example:

```
const transactionsContainer = document.
createElement('div')
transactionsContainer.setAttribute('id', 'main')
```

```
const content = document.createTextNode('Transactions')
transactionsContainer.appendChild(content)
document.body.appendChild(transactionsContainer)
const main = document.getElementById('main')
console.log(main, main.offsetWidth, main.offsetHeight)
```

Globals

In addition to classes such as `String`, `Array`, `Number`, and `Math`, which have a lot of useful methods, you can call the following methods known as globals, meaning you can invoke them from anywhere in your code:

- `encodeURI`: Encodes a Uniform Resource Identifier (URI) to give you a URL, e.g., `encodeURI('http://www.webapplog.com/js is awesome')`

- `decodeURI`: Decodes a URI

- `encodeURIComponent`: Encodes URI for URL parameters (don't use it for the entire URL string)

- `decodeURIComponent`: Decodes the fragment

- `isNaN`: Determines whether a value is a number or not

- `JSON`: Parsing (`parse()`) and serializing (`stringify()`) of JSON data

- `parseFloat`: Converts a string to a floating number

- `parseInt`: Converts a string to a number

- `Intl`: Language-specific string comparison methods

- `Error`: An error object that you can use to instantiate your own error objects; for example, `throw new Error('This book rocks!')`

- `Date`: Various methods to work with dates

JavaScript and Node.js Conventions

JavaScript uses a number of style conventions. One of them is camelCase, in which you type multiple words as one word, capitalizing the first character of the each except the first word.

Semicolons are optional. Names starting with an underscore (_) are private methods or attributes, but not because they are protected by the language. We use the underscore simply to alert the developers not to use the methods and attributes, because they may change in the future.

JavaScript supports numbers only up to 53 bits in size. Check out large numbers' libraries if you need to deal with numbers larger than that.

Another important distinction of JS is that it's a functional and prototypal language. Typical syntax for function declaration looks like this:

```js
function Sum(a,b) {
  const sum = a + b
  return sum
}
console.log(Sum(1, 2))
```

Functions in JavaScript are first-class citizens due to the functional programming nature of the language. Therefore, functions can be used as other variables or objects; for example, functions can be passed to other functions as arguments:

```js
const f = function (str1){
  return function(str2){
  return str1 + ' ' + str2
  }
}
const a = f('hello')
const b = f('goodbye')
console.log((a('Catty'))
console.log((b('Doggy'))
```

Another way to define a function is to use a fat arrow syntax. The difference is that a fat arrow will not use a name, so developers need to store the function in a variable.

```
const Sum = (a,b) => {
  const sum = a + b
  return sum
}
console.log(Sum(1, 2))
```

Another difference is that fat arrow function syntax preserves the value of `this` from the outer scope, which in a way makes the fat arrow syntax equivalent to using a bind method `bind(this)` on a regular function.

```
const Sum = function(a, b) {
  const sum = a + b
  return sum
}.bind(this)
```

Of course, in the `Sum` example we never use `this` so there's no need. But when you use classes and inheritance, you'll use `this` a lot because it's the way to refer to the class instance and its methods and attributes/fields/properties.

Speaking of instances, classes and inheritance, if you want to be a *good* full stack developer, then it's very important to know that there are several ways to instantiate an object in JS:

- Classical inheritance (`http://www.crockford.com/javascript/inheritance.html`) pattern

- Pseudo-classical inheritance (`http://javascript.info/class-patterns`) pattern

- Functional inheritance pattern

For further reading on inheritance patterns, check out "Inheritance Patterns in JavaScript" (`http://bolinfest.com/javascript/inheritance.php`) and Inheritance revisited (`https://developer.mozilla.org/en-US/docs/Web/JavaScript/Inheritance_and_the_prototype_chain`).

Mozilla Developer Network has *the* best JavaScript and DOM references (`https://developer.mozilla.org/en-US/docs/JavaScript/Reference`). Also, the VS Code editor shows autocomplete prompts and documentation hints. (No matter what, *please* stop using Notepad++.)

As for the ECMAScript specification (standard for JavaScript and Node), visit: `http://www.ecma-international.org`.

Agile Methodologies

In modern web development, in addition to full stack JavaScript most teams use Agile. The Agile software development methodology evolved due to the fact that traditional methods like Waterfall weren't good enough in situations of high unpredictability; that is, when the solution is unknown (`http://www.startuplessonslearned.com/2009/03/combining-agile-development-with.html`). Agile goes hand-in-hand with Scrum/sprint, test-driven development, continuous deployment, paired programming, and other practical techniques, many of which were borrowed from extreme programming.

Scrum

In regard to management, the Agile methodology often uses the Scrum approach. The Scrum methodology is a sequence of short cycles, and each cycle is called a *sprint*. One sprint usually lasts from one to two weeks. A typical sprint starts and ends with a sprint planning meeting where new tasks are assigned to team members. New tasks cannot be added to the sprint in progress; they can be added only at the sprint meetings.

An essential part of the Scrum methodology is the daily scrum meeting, hence the name. Each scrum is a 5-to 15-minute-long meeting, often conducted in a hallway. In scrum meetings, each team member answers three questions:

1. What have you done since yesterday?

2. What are you going to do today?

3. Do you need anything from other team members?

Like many Agile frameworks (Kanban, XP, SAFE), Scrum offers flexibility to change project requirements during development, which is a *great* improvement over the Waterfall methodology, especially in situations of high uncertainty (i.e., in startups). JavaScript is used in the UI were a lot of these changes often happen. You'll see or already see a lot of front-end teams adopting Scrum and Agile.

The advantage of Scrum methodology is that it is effective in situations where it is hard to plan ahead of time, and also in situations where a feedback loop is used as the main decision-making authority.

More about Scrum can be read at the following sources:

- Scrum Guide in PDF (`http://www.scrumguides.org/docs/scrumguide/v1/scrum-guide-us.pdf`)

- Scrum.org (`http://www.scrum.org`)

- *Succeeding with Agile* by Mike Cohen (Addison-Wesley, 2010)

Test-Driven Development

Test-driven development (TDD) consists of the following steps:

1. Write failing automated test cases for new features, tasks, or enhancement by using assertions that are either true or false.

2. Write code to successfully pass the test cases.

3. Refactor code if needed, and add functionality while keeping the test cases passed.

4. Repeat until all tasks are complete.

Tests can be split into functional and unit testing. The latter is when a system tests individual units, methods, and functions with dependencies mocked up, whereas the former (also called integration testing) is when a system tests a slice of a functionality, including dependencies.

There are several advantages of TDD:

- Fewer bugs and defects

- More efficient codebase

- Confidence that code works and doesn't break the old functionality

Continuous Deployment and Integration

Continuous deployment (CD) is a set of techniques to rapidly deliver new features, bug fixes, and enhancements to the customers. CD includes automated testing and automated deployment. Using CD, manual overhead is decreased and feedback loop time is minimized. Basically, the faster a developer can get the feedback from the customers, the sooner the product can pivot, which leads to more advantages over the competition.

Many startups deploy multiple times in a single day in comparison to the 6-to 12-month release cycle that is still typical for corporations and big companies.

The advantages of the CD approach include decreased feedback loop time and manual labor overhead.

There are Continuous Delivery, Continuous Deployment and Continuous Integration. There are differences between them but ideally you want to have all three for a faster deployment.

Some of the most popular solutions for continuous integration include the following:

- *Jenkins* (`https://jenkins.io`): An extendable open source continuous integration server

- *CircleCI* (`https://circleci.com`): Ship better code, faster

- *Travis CI* (`https://travis-ci.org`): A hosted continuous integration service for the open source community

Pair Programming

Pair programming is a technique whereby two developers work together in one environment. One of the developers is a driver, and the other is an observer. The driver writes code, and the observer assists by watching and making suggestions. Then they switch roles. The driver has a more tactical role of focusing on the current task. In contrast, the observer has a more strategic role, overseeing "the bigger picture" and finding bugs and ways to improve an algorithm.

The following are the advantages of paired programming:

- Pairs result in shorter and more effcient codebase, and introduce fewer bugs and defects.

- As an added bonus, knowledge is passed among programmers as they work together. However, conflicts between developers are possible, and not uncommon.

Back-End Definitions

The backend is another name for the server. It's everything after the browser. It includes server platforms like PHP, Python, Java, Ruby, and of course Node.js, as well as databases and other technologies.

Luckily, with modern back-end-as-a-service solutions (BaaS) you can bypass the back-end development entirely. With just a single <script> tag included, you can get a real-time database with the ability to put some logic into it like access level control (ALC), validation, and so on. There are a lot of services offered different levels of BaaS. The most popular and easy-to-use ones are Firebase and Parse (`https://firebase.google.com` and `http://parseplatform.org`).

In those cases where you still need your own custom server code, Node.js is the weapon of choice!

Node.js

Node.js is an open source, event-driven asynchronous I/O technology for building scalable and efficient web servers. Node.js consists of Google's V8 JavaScript engine and a bunch of C++ modules. A cloud company Joyent (now acquired by Samsung) maintained Node.js in the beginning, but now the open-source Node foundation oversees it.

The purpose and use of Node.js is to have non-blocking I/O which makes things faster. Non-blocking I/O is not new. It exists in NIO for Java, in Twisted for Python and in EventMachine for Ruby. The big difference is that in Node.js non-blocking I/O was built from the get-go and thus simple to use, while in other languages its a complex afterthought.

Funny enough, JavaScript wasn't even the first language for Node.js. The JavaScript implementation of Node.js was the third one after attempts at using Ruby and C++ programming languages.

Node.js is not in itself a framework like Ruby on Rails; it's more comparable to the pair of PHP and Apache. I'll provide a list of the top Node.js frameworks in Chapter 6.

The following are the advantages of using Node.js:

- Developers have high likelihood of familiarity with JavaScript due to its status as a de facto standard for web and mobile development.

- Using one language for front-end and back-end development speeds up the coding process. A developer's brain doesn't have to switch between different syntaxes, a so-called context switch. The learning of methods and classes goes faster.

- With Node.js, you could prototype quickly and go to market to do your customer development and customer acquisition early. This is an important competitive advantage over other companies that use less agile technologies (e.g., PHP and MySQL).

- Node.js is built to support real-time applications by utilizing web sockets.

Node.js evolves fast. For the current state of Node.js (as of this writing), refer to the official Node.js blog at `https://nodejs.org/en/blog`.

NoSQL and MongoDB

MongoDB, from huMONGOus, is a high-performance, no-relationship database for huge quantities of data (`https://mongodb.com`). The NoSQL concept came out when traditional relational database management systems (RDBMSs) were unable to meet the challenges of huge amounts of data.

Here are the advantages of using MongoDB:

- *Scalability*: Due to a distributed nature, multiple servers and data centers can have redundant data.

- *High performance*: MongoDB is very effective for storing and retrieving data, partially owing to the absence of relationships between elements and collections in the database.

- *Flexibility*: A key-value store is ideal for prototyping because it doesn't require developers to know the schema and there is no need for fixed data models or complex migrations.

Cloud Computing

Cloud computing consists of the following components:

- Infrastructure as a Service (IaaS), including Rackspace and Amazon Web Services

- Platform as a Service (PaaS), including Heroku and Microsoft Azure

- Back end as a Service (BaaS), the newest, coolest kid on the block, including Compose and Firebase

- Software as a Service (SaaS), including Google Apps and Salesforce.com

Cloud application platforms provide the following advantages:

- Scalability; for example, they can spawn new instances in a matter of minutes

- Ease of deployment; for example, to push to Heroku you can just use `$ git push`

- Pay-as-you-go plans where users add or remove memory and disk space based on demands

- Add-ons for easier installation and configuration of databases, app servers, packages, and so on

- Security and support

PaaS and BaaS are ideal for prototyping, building minimal viable products (MVP), and for early-stage startups in general.

Here is the list of the most popular PaaS solutions:

- Heroku (`https://heroku.com`)

- AWS Elastic Beanstalk (`https://aws.amazon.com/elasticbeanstalk`)

- Microsoft Azure (`https://azure.microsoft.com`)

HTTP Requests and Responses

Each HTTP Request and Response consists of the following components:

- *Header:* Information about encoding, length of the body, origin, content type, and so on

- *Body:* Content, usually parameters or data, that is passed to the server or sent back to a client

In addition, the HTTP Request contains these elements:

- *Method:* There are several methods, with the most common being GET, POST, PUT, and DELETE

- *URL:* Protocol, host, port, path; for example, `https://webaplog.com/es6`

- *Query string:* Everything after a question mark in the URL (e.g., `?q=rpjs&page=20`)

RESTful API

RESTful (REpresentational State Transfer) APIs became popular due to the demand in distributed systems to become stateless because stateless apps are better to scale. This turned into a demand for each transaction/request to include enough information about the state of the client. In a sense, this standard is stateless because no information about the clients' states is stored on the server, thus making it possible for each request to be served by a different system.

Here are some of the distinct characteristics of RESTful APIs:

- It has better scalability support due to the fact that different components can be independently deployed to different servers.

- It is easier to use than to use Simple Object Access Protocol (SOAP) because of the simpler verb and noun structure in REST, that's no need for a verb in the URL.

- It uses HTTP methods such as GET, POST, DELETE, PUT, OPTIONS, and so on.

Table 1-1 is an example of a simple Create, Read, Update, and Delete (CRUD) RESTful API for Message Collection.

Table 1-1. *An Example of a CRUD RESTful API*

Method	URL	Meaning
GET	`/messages.json`	Return list of messages in JSON format
PUT	`/messages.json`	Update/replace all messages and return status/error in JSON
POST	`/messages.json`	Create new message and return its ID in JSON format
GET	`/messages/{id}.json`	Return message that has ID `{id}` in JSON format
PUT	`/messages/{id}.json`	Replace message that has ID `{id}` with payload
PATCH	`/messages/{id}.json`	Update message that has ID `{id}` with payload
DELETE	`/messages/{id}.json`	Delete message that has ID `{id}`

REST is not a protocol; it is an architecture in the sense that it's more flexible than SOAP, which is a protocol. Therefore, REST API URLs could look like `/messages/list.html` or `/messages/list.xml` in case we want to support these formats. But most of the time, developers just use JSON without any extensions: `/messages` and `/messages/{id}`.

PUT and DELETE are idempotent methods, which means that if the server receives two or more similar requests, the end result will be the same. On the other hand, the GET method is nullipotent because the read operation is safe on repeats. However, POST is not idempotent because it will affect state and cause side effects on repeats.

We will use REST in the next chapters for building Node.js backend and Backbone client.

Summary

This concludes the first chapter. In this chapter we've covered some of the core concepts of web development. They'll be a solid foundation for the rest of the book. I'm sure some of the concepts were familiar to you:

- HTML
- CSS
- JavaScript types and objects
- Agile
- Node.js
- NoSQL
- HTTP Request
- RESTful API

Nevertheless, it's good to brush up on them because they are numerous and vast. Theory is not that useful or interesting without understanding how it applies and benefits the actual code. Therefore, we'll move swiftly to the technical setup to get you to the coding projects fast.

CHAPTER 2

Setup

One of my most productive days was throwing away 1,000 lines of code.

—Ken Thompson

In this chapter, we'll cover the following topics:

- Suggestions for the toolset

- Step-by-step installation of local components

- Preparation for the use of cloud services

The proper setup is absolutely crucial to your productive development. You need to have everything ready when you embark on a long journey, right? The two important things to install are dependencies and the toolset. Dependencies are absolutely necessary and technologies like Node.js or MongoDB. Moreover, the toolset is highly recommended because it will make you more productive. They enable the server-side code and persistence, respectively. In addition to that, in the cloud section, we cover setup of the services for deployment and development. They will enable you to keep your code under version control and deploy it in a scalable manner.

© Azat Mardan 2018
A. Mardan, *Full Stack JavaScript*, https://doi.org/10.1007/978-1-4842-3718-2_2

Local Setup

Local setup is what we use on our development machines when we work on a project. It includes anything from folders, browsers, editors, and HTTP servers to databases. Figure 2-1 shows an example of the initial development environment setup.

Development Folder

If you don't have a specific development folder for your web development projects, you could create a `Development` folder in the `Documents` folder (path will be `Documents/Development`). To work on the code example, create a `fullstack-javascript` folder inside your web development projects folder; for example, if you create a `fullstack-javascript` folder inside of the `Development` folder, the path will be `Documents/Development/fullstack-javascript`. You could use the Finder app on macOS or the following terminal commands on Posix (macOS X/Linux) systems:

```
$ cd ~/Documents
$ mkdir Development
$ cd Development
$ mkdir fullstack-javascript
```

Figure 2-1. *Initial development environment setup*

> **Tip**   To open macOS Finder app in the current directory from
> Terminal, just type and run the $ open. command. On Windows,
> Terminal is command prompt.

To get the list of files and folders, use this UNIX/Linux command:

```
$ ls
```

or to display hidden files and folders, like.git, use this:

```
$ ls -lah
```

Another alternative to $ ls is $ ls -alt. The difference between the
-lah and the -alt options is that the latter sorts items chronologically and
the former sorts them alphabetically.

You can use the Tab key to autocomplete names of the files and folders.

Later, you could copy examples into the `fullstack-javascript`
folder as well as create apps in that folder.

> **Tip**   Another useful thing is to have the New Terminal at Folder
> option in Finder on macOS. To enable it, open your System
> Preferences (you could use Command + Space, a.k.a. Spotlight,
> for it). Find Keyboard and click it. Open Keyboard Shortcuts and click
> Services. Select the New Terminal at Folder and New Terminal Tab at
> Folder check boxes. Close the window (optional).

Browsers

I recommend downloading the latest version of the WebKit or Gecko browser of your choice:

- Chrome (`https://www.google.com/chrome`) (recommended)

- Safari (`https://www.apple.com/safari`)

- Firefox (`https://www.mozilla.org/en-US/ firefox/new`)

Whereas Chrome (Figure 2-2) and Safari already come with built-in developer tools, you'll need the Firebug plug-in for Firefox.

Figure 2-2. *Chrome Developer Tools in action*

Firebug and developer tools allow developers to do many things, including these:

- Debug JavaScript

- Manipulate HTML and DOM elements

- Modify CSS on the fly

- Monitor HTTP requests and responses

- Run profiles and inspect heap dumps

- See loaded assets such as images, CSS, and JS files

There are some great Chrome Developer Tools (DevTools) tutorials, such as the following:

- Explore and Master Chrome DevTools (`https://discover-devtools.codeschool.com`) with Code School

- Chrome DevTools videos (`https://developers.google.com/chrome-developer-tools/docs/videos`)

- Chrome DevTools overview (`https://developers.google.com/chrome-developer-tools`)

IDEs and Text Editors

One of the best things about JavaScript is that you don't need to compile the code. Because JS lives in and is run in a browser, you can do debugging right there, in a browser! It's an interpreted language, not a compiled one. Therefore, I highly recommend a lightweight text editor instead of a full-blown integrated development environment, or IDE, but if you are already familiar and comfortable with the IDE of your choice like Eclipse (`http://www.eclipse.org`), NetBeans (`https://netbeans.org`), or Aptana (`http://aptana.com`), feel free to stick with it.

Here is a list of the most popular text editors and IDEs used in web development:

- *VS Code* (`https://www.visualstudio.com/features/node-js-vs`): Node.js tools for the famous Visual Studio environment from a small Redmond, Washington-based software startup company.

- *Atom* (`https://atom.io`): A web editor built on web technologies from the creators of GitHub, the world's largest code storage and collaboration space.

- *Sublime Text* (`https://www.sublimetext.com`): macOS and Windows versions are available. This is an even better alternative to TextMate, with an unlimited evaluation period.

- *Coda* (`http://panic.com/coda`): All-in-one editor with FTP browser and preview, has support for development with and on an iPad.

- *Aptana Studio* (`http://aptana.com`): Full-sized IDE with a built-in terminal and many other tools.

- *WebStorm* (`http://www.jetbrains.com/webstorm`): Feature-rich IDE that allows for Node.js debugging. It is developed by JetBrains and marketed as the smartest JavaScript IDE.

Please, please, please don't use Vim, TextEdit or Notepad++! Having code coloring and parentheses matching will make a great difference when typing and debugging.

Version Control Systems

A version control system is a must-have even in projects with a single developer because such a system keep all the history which makes it easy to restore code or revert changes. Git is the most popular version control system.

Also, many cloud services (e.g., Heroku) require Git for deployment. I also highly recommend getting used to Git and Git terminal commands instead of using Git visual clients and apps with a GUI: GitX (`http://gitx.frim.nl`), Gitbox (`http://www.gitboxapp.com`), or GitHub for Desktop (`https://desktop.github.com`).

Subversion is a nondistributed version control system. This article compares Git vs. Subversion: `https://git.wiki.kernel.org/index.php/GitSvnComparison`.

Here are the steps to install and set up Git on your machine:

1. Download the latest version for your OS at `https://git-scm.com/downloads`.

2. Install Git from the downloaded `\*.dmg` package; that is, run the `\*.pkg` file and follow the wizard.

3. Find the Terminal app by using Command + Space, a.k.a. Spotlight, on macOS. For Windows you could use PuTTY (`http://www.chiark.greenend.org.uk/~sgtatham/putty`) or Cygwin (`http://www.cygwin.com`).

4. In your terminal, type these commands, substituting "John Doe" and johndoe@example.com with your name and e-mail:

```
$ git config --global user.name
"John Doe"
$ git config --global user.email
johndoe@example.com
```

45

5. To check the installation, run this command:

```
$ git version
```

6. You should see something like this in your terminal window (your version might vary; in my case it's 1.8.3.2):

```
git version 2.14.3 (Apple Git-98)
```

Generating SSH keys and uploading them to SaaS/PaaS web sites will be covered later.

Local HTTP Servers

Although you can do most of the front-end development without a local HTTP server, it is needed for loading files with HTTP Requests/AJAX calls. Also, it's just good practice in general to use a local HTTP server. This way, your development environment is as close to the production environment as possible.

I recommend you use Node-based tools as static web servers. They lack GUIs, but they are simple and fast. You can install them with npm (comes with Node.js; instructions are later in this chapter):

- *node-static* (`https://github.com/cloudhead/node-static`): Static file server with built-in caching. Run `npm i -g node-static` to install.

- *http-server* (`https://www.npmjs.com/package/http-server`): Zero-configuration command-line HTTP server. Run `npm i -g htt-server` to install.

If you prefer something with GUIs to a command-line interface (CLI), you might want to consider the following modifications of the Apache web server. MAMP, MAMP Stack, and XAMPP have intuitive GUIs that allow you to change configurations and host file settings.

- *XAMPP* (`https://www.apachefriends.org`): Apache distribution containing MySQL, PHP and Perl for Windows, macOS, Linux, and Solaris.

- *MAMP* (`https://www.mamp.info`): Apache, MySQL, and PHP personal web server for macOS.

- *MAMP Stack* (`https://bitnami.com/stack/mamp`): Another Apache, MySQL, and PHP stack for macOS.

Database: MongoDB

The following steps are better suited for macOS/Linux-based systems, but with some modification they can be used for Windows systems as well (i.e., `$PATH` variable, Step 3). Here I describe the MongoDB installation from the official package, because I found that this approach is more robust and leads to less conflicts. However, there are many other ways to install it on macOS (`https://docs.mongodb.com/manual/tutorial/install-mongodb-on-os-x`), for example using Brew, as well as on other systems (`http://docs.mongodb.com/manual/installation`).

1. Download MongoDB from `http://www.mongodb.com/download-center#community`. For the latest Apple laptops, like MacBook, select macOS X 64-bit version. The owners of older Macs should browse the link at `http://dl.mongodb.com/dl/osx/i386`

Tip   To figure out the architecture type of your processor, type the $ uname -p at the command line.

---

2. Unpack the package into your web development
    folder (`~/Documents/Development` or any other).
    If you want, you could install MongoDB into the
    `/usr/local/mongodb` folder.

3. Optional: If you would like to access MongoDB
    commands from anywhere on your system, you need
    to add your `mongodb` path to the `$PATH` variable. For
    macOS, open system `/etc/paths` file with:

    ```
    sudo vi /etc/paths
    ```

    or, if you prefer VS Code:

    ```
    code /etc/paths
    ```

    And add this line to the /etc/paths file:

    ```
    /usr/local/mongodb/bin
    ```

4. Create a `data` folder; by default, MongoDB uses
    `/data/db`. Please note that this might be different
    in new versions of MongoDB. To create it, type and
    execute the following commands in the terminal:

    ```
    $ sudo mkdir -p /data/db
    $ sudo chown id -u /data/db
    ```

    If you prefer to use a path other than `/data/db`
    you could specify it using the `--dbpath` option to
    `mongod` (the main MongoDB service).

5. Go to the folder where you unpacked MongoDB. That location should have a bin folder in it. From there, type the following command in your terminal:

    ```
    $./bin/mongod
    ```

6. If you see something like the following (and as in Figure 2-3) it means that the MongoDB database server is running:

    ```
    MongoDB starting: pid =7218
    port=27017...
    ```

    By default, it's listening at `http://localhost:27017`. If you go to your browser and type `http://localhost:28017` you should be able to see the version number, logs, and other useful information. In this case the MondoDB server is using two different ports (27017 and 28017): One is primary (native) for the communications with apps and the other is a web-based GUI for monitoring and statistics. In our Node.js code we'll be using only 27017. Don't forget to restart the Terminal window after adding a new path to the `$PATH` variable.

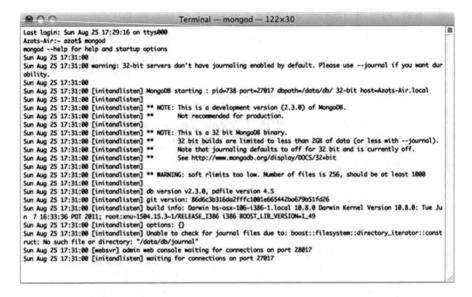

Figure 2-3. *Starting up the MongoDB server*

Now, to take it even further, we can test to determine if we have access to the MongoDB console/shell, which will act as a client to this server. This means that we'll have to keep the terminal window with the server open and running.

7. Open another terminal window at the same folder and execute:

```
$ ./bin/mongo
```

You should see something like "MongoDB shell version..."

8. Then type and execute:

```
> db.test.save( { a: 1 } )
> db.test.find()
```

If you see that your record is being saved, then everything went well (Figure 2-4).

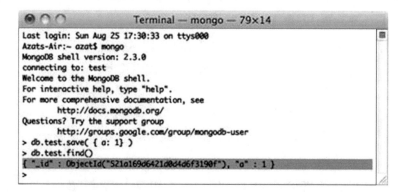

Figure 2-4. Running MongoDB client and storing sample data

Commands `find` and `save` do exactly what you might think they do.

The official MongoDB website has the detailed instructions for installing MongoDB on macOS at: `http://docs.mongodb.com/manual/tutorial/install-mongodb-on-os-x`. TK

Note   MAMP and XAMPP applications come with MySQL—an open source traditional SQL database—and phpMyAdmin—a web interface for MySQL database.

On macOS (and most UNIX systems), to close the process use Control + C. If you use Control + Z it will put the process to sleep (or detach the terminal window); in this case, you might end up with the lock on data files and will have to use the `kill` command or Activity Monitor, and manually delete the locked file in the data folder. In vanilla Mac.

Terminal Command +. is an alternative to Control + C.

Required Components

The following are required technologies. Please make sure you have them before proceeding to the next chapter.

1. *Node.js*: We need it for build tools and back-end apps. Get the version that has LTS even if the number is lower than the current NON-LTS version, because the LTS versions have longer support period: `https://nodejs.org`.

2. *npm*: The Node.js package manager that comes bundled with Node.js (no need to install anything extra).

3. *Browser JS libraries*: We need them for front-end apps.

I highly recommend installing other optional but useful components:

1. *nvm*: The Node.js version manager, which allows to switch between Node.js versions quickly.

2. *Compass*: A desktop client GUI app for working with MongoDB as a replacement of the Mongo shell/REPL. `https://www.mongodb.com/products/compass`

Node.js Installation

Node.js is available at `https://nodejs.org/#download` (Figure 2-5). The installation is trivial: Download the archive and run the `*.pkg` package installer. To check the installation of Node.js, you could type and execute:

```
$ node -v
```

I use v8.11.1 for this book and tested all examples with v8.11.1. If you use another version, do so at your own risk. I cannot guarantee that the examples will run.

Assuming you have 8.11.1, it should show something similar to this: `v8.11.1`.

If you want to switch between multiple versions of Node.js, there are solutions for that:

- *nvm* (`https://github.com/creationix/nvm`): Node.js Version Manager

- *Nave* (`https://github.com/isaacs/nave`): Virtual environments for Node.js

- *n* (`https://github.com/tj/n`): Node.js version management

The Node.js package already includes npm—Node.js Package Manager (`https://npmjs.org`). We'll use npm extensively to install Node.js modules.

Node.js® is a JavaScript runtime built on Chrome's V8 JavaScript engine. Node.js uses an event-driven, non-blocking I/O model that makes it lightweight and efficient. Node.js' package ecosystem, npm, is the largest ecosystem of open source libraries in the world.

Important March 2018 security upgrades now available

Download for macOS (x64)

8.11.1 LTS	9.10.1 Current
Recommended For Most Users	Latest Features

Other Downloads | Changelog | API Docs   Other Downloads | Changelog | API Docs

Or have a look at the LTS schedule.

Sign up for Node.js Everywhere, the official Node.js Weekly Newsletter.

Figure 2-5. *Node.js home page that shows LTS and non-LTS versions*

Browser JavaScript Libraries

Front-end JavaScript libraries are downloaded and unpacked from their respective web sites. Those files are usually put in the Development folder (e.g., `~/Documents/Development`) for future use. Often, there is a choice between the minified production version (more on that in the AMD and Require.js section of Chapter 4) and a version that is extensively rich development comments.

Another approach is to hot-link these scripts from CDNs such as Google Hosted Libraries (`https://developers.google.com/speed/libraries/devguide`), CDNJS (`https://cdnjs.com`), Microsoft Ajax Content Delivery Network (`https://docs.microsoft.com/en-us/aspnet/ajax/cdn/overview`), and others. By doing so the apps will be faster for some users, but won't work locally at all without the Internet.

Speaking of dependencies, I recommend downloading the following libraries that will be used in the book's project. To keep things simple, we will use just simple `.js` or `.min.js` files and not the npm packages:

- Bootstrap is a CSS/Less framework. It's available at `https://getbootstrap.com`.

- jQuery is available at `https://jquery.com`.

- Backbone.js is available at `https://backbonejs.org`.

- Underscore.js is available at `https://underscorejs.org`.

- Require.js is available at `https://requirejs.org`.

Less App

Less as a front-end interpreter is available at lesscss.org. You could unpack it into your development folder (`~/Documents/Development`) or any other folder.

The Less App is a macOS application for "on-the-fly" compilation of Less to CSS. It's available at incident57.com/less.

Cloud Setup

The cloud setup discussed in the following sections will allow you to keep your code under version control and deploy it in a scalable manner.

SSH Keys

For GitHub repositories, developers have to enter username and password every time with HTTPS URLs (looks like `https://github.com/azat-co/fullstack-javascript.git`), unless they use a keychain. SSH keys provide a secure connection without the need to enter a user name and password every time. The SSH URLs look like `git@github.com:azat-co/fullstack-javascript.git`.

To generate SSH keys for GitHub on macOS/UNIX machines, do the following:

1. Check for existing SSH keys:

    ```
    $ cd ~/.ssh
    $ ls -lah
    ```

2. If you see some files like `id_rsa` (please refer to Figure 2-6 for an example), you could delete them or back them up into a separate folder by using the following commands:

    ```
    $ mkdir key_backup
    $ cp id_rsa* key_backup
    $ rm id_rsa*
    ```

3. Now generate a new SSH key pair using the `ssh-keygen` command, assuming you are in the `~/.ssh` folder:

    ```
    $ ssh-keygen -t rsa -C
    "your_email@youremail.com"
    ```

4. Answer the questions; it is better to keep the default name of `id_rsa`. Then copy the content of the `id_rsa.pub` file to your clipboard (Figure 2-6):

    ```
    $ pbcopy < ~/.ssh/id_rsa.pub
    ```

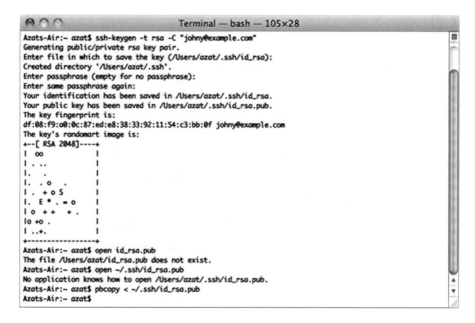

Figure 2-6. *Generating RSA key for SSH and copying public key to clipboard*

5. Alternatively, open `id_rsa.pub` file in the default editor:

```
$ edit id_rsa.pub
```

Or in VS Code (recommended):

```
$ code id_rsa.pub
```

GitHub

The next steps will show how to connect to GitHub (think of it as a versioned code storage) using SSH and SSH keys:

1. After you have copied the public key, go to `https://github.com`, log in, go to your account settings, select SSH Key, and add the new SSH key. Assign a name, such as the name of your computer, and paste the value of your public key.

2. To check if you have an SSH connection to GitHub, type and execute the following command in your terminal:

    ```
    $ ssh -T git@github.com
    ```

    If you see something like this:

    ```
    Hi your-GitHub-username! You've successfully
    authenticated, but GitHub does not provide shell
    access.
    ```

    then everything is set up.

3. The first time you connect to GitHub, you may receive a message "Authenticity of Host ... Can't Be Established warning". Please don't be alarmed with such a message. It confirms that the host you are trying to connect to is trusted. Simply proceed by answering "Yes" as shown in Figure 2-7.

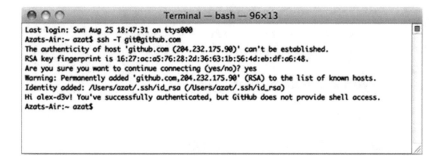

Figure 2-7. *Testing SSH connection to GitHub for the first time*

If for some reason you have a different message, please repeat Steps 3 and 4 from the previous section on SSH keys or reupload the content of your `*.pub` file to GitHub.

`Warning Keep your id_rsa file private and don't share it with anybody!`

More instructions are available at GitHub: Generating SSH Keys (`https://helpgithub.com/articles/generating-ssh-keys`). TK

Windows users might find the SSH key generator feature in PuTTY useful.

Microsoft Azure

Here are the steps to set up a Microsoft Azure account:

1. You'll need to sign up for Microsoft Azure Web Site and Virtual Machine previews. Currently Microsoft has a 90-day free trial available at `https://azure.microsoft.com/en-us`.

2. Enable Git Deployment and create a user name and password, then upload the SSH public key to Microsoft Azure.

3. Install the Node.js SDK, which is available at `https://azure.microsoft.com/en-us/develop/nodejs`. TK

4. To check your installation type:

```
$ azure -v
```

You should see something like this:

```
Microsoft Azure: Microsoft's Cloud Platform...
Tool Version 0.6.0
```

5. Log in to Microsoft Azure Portal at `https://azure.microsoft.com` (Figure 2-8).

Figure 2-8. *Registering on Microsoft Azure*

6. Select New, then select Web Site, and Quick Create. Type the name that will serve as the URL for your web site, and click OK.

7. Go to this newly created web site's Dashboard and
    select Set Up Git Publishing. Come up with a user
    name and password. This combination can be
    used to deploy to any web site in your subscription,
    meaning that you do not need to set credentials for
    every web site you create. Click OK.

8. On the follow-up screen, it should show you the Git
    URL to push to, something like this:

    ```
    https://azatazure@azat.scm.azurewebsites.
    net/azat.git
    ```

    You will also see instructions on how to proceed
    with deployment. We'll cover them later.

9. Advanced user option: Follow this tutorial to
    create a virtual machine and install MongoDB on
    it: Install MongoDB on a virtual machine running
    CentOS Linux in Microsoft Azure (`https://www.`
    `windowsazure.com/en-us/manage/linux/`
    `common-tasks/mongodb-on-a-linux-vm`).

Heroku

Heroku is a polyglot agile application deployment platform (see `https://`
`www.heroku.com`). Heroku works similarly to Microsoft Azure in the sense
that you can use Git to deploy applications. There is no need to install
Virtual Machine for MongoDB because Heroku has a MongoHQ add-on
(`https://addons.heroku.com/mongohq`).

To set up Heroku, follow these steps:

1. Sign up at `https://heroku.com`. Currently they have a free account; to use it, select all options as minimum (0) and database as shared.

2. Download Heroku Toolbelt at (`https://toolbelt.heroku.com`). Toolbelt is a package of tools; that is, libraries that consist of Heroku, Git, and Foreman (`https://github.com/ddollar/foreman`). For users of older Macs, get this client (`https://github.com/heroku/heroku`) directly. If you utilize another OS, browse Heroku Client GitHub (`https://github.com/heroku/heroku`).

3. After the installation is done, you should have access to the `heroku` command. To check it and log in to Heroku, type:

```
$ heroku login
```

It will ask you for Heroku credentials (user name and password), and if you've already created the SSH key, it will automatically upload it to the Heroku web site (Figure 2-9).

Figure 2-9. *The response to the successful $ heroku login command*

4. If everything went well, to create a Heroku
    application inside of your specific project folder, you
    should be able to run this command:

```
$ heroku create
```

More instructions for getting started with Node.js and other languages
are available from Heroku at `https://devcenter.heroku.com/start`.

Summary

In this chapter, we've covered the technical setup of the version control
system, cloud clients, and the installation of various tools and libraries.
We'll use these libraries and tools throughout the book, for this reason it's
important to have them installed and ready to go. In addition, the chapter
provided a few links to external resources that will help you understand
and learn web development tools better. One of the most useful of such
resources is DevTools.

You must be dying to get started with the actual coding. The wait is
over. Meet the first full stack JavaScript code in the next chapter.

PART II

Front-End Prototyping

CHAPTER 3

Getting Data from Backend Using jQuery and Parse

There are two ways of constructing a software design: One way is to make it so simple that there are obviously no deficiencies, and the other way is to make it so complicated that there are no obvious deficiencies. The first method is far more difficult.

—Tony Hoare

This chapter covers the following topics:

- Definitions of JSON, AJAX, and CORS

- Overview of main jQuery functions

- Bootstrap scaffolding

- Main Less components

- Illustrations of JSONP calls on OpenWeatherMap API example

- Parse overview

© Azat Mardan 2018
A. Mardan, *Full Stack JavaScript*, https://doi.org/10.1007/978-1-4842-3718-2_3

- Explanations on how to build a Message Board front-end-only application with jQuery and Parse

- Step-by-step instructions on deployment to Microsoft Azure and Heroku

- Updating and deleting of messages

This chapter is a basic introduction to front-end web development. It covers things important to front-end development of apps such as Bootstrap and Less. These amazing libraries allow developers to have a nice user interface in no time.

This chapter also covers the terminology and explains JSON, AJAX, and CORS. We then explore the example of a weather app.

We use Parse as our backend to streamline things and make development faster while still keeping it realistic. The cornerstone of this chapter is a persistent message board application built with Parse and jQuery.

Definitions

Before anything else, let's clarify some terms. They are important enough for us to pause and get familiar with them. If these are familiar to you, you might want to skip ahead.

JavaScript Object Notation

Here is the definition of JavaScript Object Notation (JSON) from `http://www.json.org`.

> *JavaScript Object Notation, or JSON, is a lightweight data-interchange format. It is easy for humans to read and write. It is easy for machines to parse and generate. It is based on a subset of the JavaScript Programming Language, Standard ECMA-262* (`http://www.ecma-international.org/publications/files/ECMA-ST/Ecma-262.pdf`).

JSON is a text format that is completely language independent but uses conventions that are familiar to programmers of the C-family of languages, including C, C++, C#, Java, JavaScript, Perl, Python, and many others. These properties make JSON an ideal data-interchange language.

JSON has become a standard for transferring data between different components of web and mobile applications and third-party services. JSON is also widely used inside the applications as a format for configuration, locales, translation files, or any other data.

A typical JSON object looks like this:

```
{
  "a": "value of a",
  "b": "value of b"
}
```

We have an object with key/value pairs. Keys are on the left and values are on the right side of colons (:). In computer science terminology, JSON is equivalent to a hash table, a keyed list, or an associative array (depending on the particular language). The only big difference between JSON and JS object literal notation (native JS objects) is that JSON is more stringent and requires double quotes (") for key identifiers and string values. Both types can be serialized into a string representation with JSON. stringify() and deserialized with JSON.parse(), assuming we have a valid JSON object in a string format.

However, every member of an object can be an array, primitive, or another object; for example:

```
{
    "posts": [{
        "title": "Get your mind in shape!",
        "votes": 9,
```

```
    "comments": [
        "nice!",
        "good link"
    ]}, {
    "title": "Yet another post",
    "votes": 0,
    "comments": []
  }],
  "totalPosts": 2
}
```

In this example, we have an object with the `posts` property. The value of the `posts` property is an array of objects, each of which has `title`, `votes`, and `comments` keys. The `votes` property holds a number primitive, whereas `comments` is an array of strings. We cannot have functions as fields. JSON is strictly a data structure. (We can have functions in JS objects though.)

JSON is much more flexible and compact than XML or other data formats, as outlined in this article: "JSON: The Fat-Free Alternative to XML" (`www.json.org/xml.html`). Conveniently, MongoDB uses a JSON-like format called Binary JSON (`http://bsonspec.org`) (BSON), discussed further in the Chapter 7 section BSON.

AJAX

Asynchronous JavaScript and XML (AJAX) is used on the client side (browser) to send and receive data from the server by utilizing an `XMLHttpRequest` object in JavaScript language. Despite the name, the use of XML is not required, and JSON is often used instead. That's why developers almost never say AJAX anymore. Keep in mind that HTTP requests could be made synchronously, but it's not a good practice to do so. The most typical example of a sync request would be the `<script>` tag inclusion.

Cross-Domain Calls

For security reasons, the implementation of an `XMLHTTPRequest` object does not allow for cross-domain calls, that is when a client-side code and a server-side one are on different domains. There are methods to work around this issue.

One of them is to use JSONP (`https://en.wikipedia.org/wiki/JSONP`), JSON with padding/prefix. It's basically a dynamic manipulation via DOM-generated `<script>` tags. The `<script>` tags don't fall into the same domain limitation. The JSONP request includes the name of a callback function in a request query string. For example, the `jQuery.ajax()` function automatically generates a unique function name and appends it to the request (which is one string broken into multiple lines for readability):

```
https://graph.facebook.com/search
    ?type=post
    &limit=20
    &q=Gatsby
    &callback=jQuery16207184716751798987_1368412972614
    &_=1368412984735
```

The second approach is to use cross-origin resource sharing (CORS: `https://www.w3.org/TR/cors`), which is a better solution, but it requires control over the server side to modify response headers. We use this technique in the final version of the Message Board example application, which we build throughout the book. Here is an example of a CORS server response header:

```
Access-Control-Allow-Origin: *
```

More about CORS is available on the Resources tab of the Enable CORS website (`https://enable-cors.org/resources.html`) and in the article "Using CORS" by Monsur Hossain (`https://www.html5rocks.com/en/tutorials/cors`). You can test CORS requests at `http://test-cors.org`.

If some server does not support CORS but you want to use its API, then you can use this amazing proxy service `https://cors-anywhere.herokuapp.com`. To use it, simple append your non-CORS API URL to the `https://cors-anywhere.herokuapp.com/`. For example, to fetch the weather forecast Montevideo, Uruguay via the proxy, use this URL in `fetch()`, `XHR` or other browser library (won't work when just navigating in the browser and may not work because of the invalidated API key in the future): `https://cors-anywhere.herokuapp.com/https://api.openweathermap.org/data/2.5/forecast?q=montevideo,uy&appid=cb7c76071b4d2f7f2baf9dd426181785&units=metric`.

jQuery Functions

Throughout the book we'll be using jQuery (`http://jquery.com`) for DOM manipulations, HTTP Requests, and JSONP calls. React is a more modern technology and I wrote one of the biggest and most comprehensive books on it called React Quickly (Manning, 2017). But jQuery is still very popular and wide-spread. I can even say that jQuery became a de facto standard of the web development because of a straightforward yet versatile and powerful API and a rich collection of UI widgets. jQuery uses the `$` object or function, which is a selector and which provides a simple yet efficient way to access any HTML DOM element on a page by its ID, class, tag name, attribute value, structure, or any combination thereof. The syntax is very similar to CSS, where we use # for id and . for class selection. For example:

```
$('#main').hide()
$('p.large').attr('style','color:red')
$('#main').show().html('<div>new div</div>')
```

Here is the list of most commonly used jQuery API functions, full description for which are available at `http://api.jquery.com`:

- `find()`: Selects elements based on the provided selector string

- `hide()` Hides an element if it was visible

- `show()` Shows an element if it was hidden

- `html()` Gets or sets an inner HTML (content) of an element

- `append()` Injects an element into the DOM after the selected element

- `prepend()` Injects an element into the DOM before the selected element

- `on()` Attaches an event listener to an element

- `off()` Detaches an event listener from an element

- `css()` Gets or sets the style attribute value of an element

- `attr()` Gets or sets any attribute of an element

- `val()` Gets or sets the value attribute of an element

- `text()` Gets the combined text of an element and its children

- `each()` Iterates over a set of matched elements

Most jQuery functions act not only on a single element, on which they are called, but on a set of matched elements if the result of the selection has multiple items. This is a common pitfall that leads to bugs, and it usually happens when a jQuery selector is too broad.

Also, jQuery has many available plug-ins and libraries that provide a rich user interface or other functionality. For example:

- jQuery UI (`http://jqueryui.com`)
- jQuery Mobile (`http://jquerymobile.com`)

Bootstrap

This section explains how to set up the Bootstrap scaffolding for the projects in the book. What is Bootstrap? Bootstrap (`http://getbootstrap.com`), or Twitter Bootstrap, is a collection of CSS/Less rules and JavaScript plug-ins for creating a good user interface and user experience without spending a lot of time on such details as rounded-edge buttons, cross-compatibility, responsiveness, and so on. This collection or framework is perfect for rapid prototyping of your ideas. Nevertheless, due to its ability to be customized, Bootstrap is also a good foundation for serious projects. The source code is written in Less (`http://lesscss.org`), but plain CSS can be downloaded and used as well.

Here is a simple example of using Bootstrap scaffolding for the version v4.0.0-alpha. The structure of the project should look like this:

```
/01-bootstrap
  -index.html
  /css
    -bootstrap.css
    -bootstrap.min.css
    ... (other files if needed)
  /js
    -bootstrap.js
    -bootstrap.min.js
    -npm.js
```

First let's create the `index.html` file with proper tags:

```
<!DOCTYPE html>
<html lang="en">
  <head>

  </head>
  <body>
  </body>
</html>
```

Include the Bootstrap library as a minified CSS file:

```
<!DOCTYPE html>
<html lang="en">
  <head>
    <link
      type="text/css"
      rel="stylesheet"
      href="css/bootstrap.min.css" />
  </head>
  <body>
  </body>
</html>
```

Apply scaffolding with `container-fluid` and `row-fluid` classes:

```
<body>
  <div class="container-fluid">
    <div class="row-fluid">
    </div> *<!--row-fluid -->*
  </div> *<!-- container-fluid -->*
</body>
```

Bootstrap uses a 12-column grid. The size of an individual cell could be specified by classes `col-size-N`, for example, `col-sm-1`, `col-lg-1`, `col-md-6`. There are also classes `offset-size-N`, for example, `offset-md-3`, `offset-lg-1`, ... `offset-sm-6`, to move cells to the right.

We'll use the `col-md-12` and `hero-unit` classes for the main content block:

```
<div class="row-fluid">
  <div class="col-md-12">
    <div id="content">
      <div class="row-fluid">
        <div class="col-md-12">
          <div class="hero-unit">
            <h1>
              Welcome to Super
              Simple Backbone
              Starter Kit
            </h1>
            <p>
              This is your home page.
              To edit it just modify
              the <i>index.html</i> file!
            </p>
            <p>
              <a
                class="btn btn-primary btn-large"
                href="http://twitter.github.com/bootstrap"
                target="_blank">
                Learn more
              </a>
            </p>
```

```
        </div> *<!-- hero-unit -->*
      </div> *<!-- col-md-12 -->*
    </div> *<!-- row-fluid -->*
  </div> *<!-- content -->*
</div> *<!-- col-md-12 -->*
</div> *<!-- row-fluid -->*
```

This is the full source code of the index.html from the 1-bootstrap folder (http://bit.ly/2JCbSTv):

```html
<!DOCTYPE html>
<html lang="en">
  <head>
    <link type="text/css" rel="stylesheet" href="css/
    bootstrap.css" />
  </head>
  <body >
    <div class="container-fluid">
      <div class="row-fluid">
        <div class="col-md-12">
          <div id="content">
            <div class="row-fluid">
              <div class="col-md-12">
                <div class="hero-unit">
                  <h1>Welcome to Super Simple Backbone
                  Starter Kit</h1>
                  <p>This is your home page. To edit it
                  just modify <i>index.html</i> file!</p>
                  <p><a class="btn btn-primary btn-
                  large" href="http://twitter.github.com/
                  bootstrap" target="_blank" >Learn more
                  </a></p>
                </div> *<!-- hero-unit -->*
```

```
        </div> *<!-- col-md-12 -->*
       </div> *<!-- row-fluid -->*
      </div> *<!-- content -->*
     </div> *<!-- col-md-12 -->*
    </div> *<!-- row-fluid -->*
   </div> *<!-- container-fluid -->*
  </body>
</html>
```

This example is available for downloading and pulling from the GitHub public repository at `https://github.com/azat-co/fullstack-javascript` under the 01-bootstrap folder (`http://bit.ly/2JCbSTv`).

CSS is not a real programming language. It does not have a dependency mechanism, variables or functions. That's why some developers invented CSS frameworks and a lot of developers use them to much success over plain CSS. Their frameworks allow for a better CSS reuse and composition. Here are some other useful tools—CSS frameworks and CSS preprocessors—worth checking out:

- *Compass*: CSS framework (`https://compass-style.org`)

- *Sass*: Extension of CSS3 and analog to Less (`https://sass-lang.com`)

- *Blueprint*: CSS framework (`https://blueprintcss.io`)

- *Foundation*: Responsive front-end framework (`https://foundation.zurb.com`)

- *Bootswatch*: Collection of customized Bootstrap themes (`http://bootswatch.com`)

- *WrapBootstrap*: Marketplace for customized Bootstrap themes (`https://wrapbootstrap.com`)

To work with the Bootstrap source files or its theme files, you need to use Less or Sass.

Less

Less is a dynamic stylesheet language. Less has variables, mix-ins, and operators that make it faster for developers to reuse CSS rules. Sometimes, and in this case, it's true that less is more and more is less. A browser cannot interpret Less syntax, so Less source code must be compiled to CSS in one of three ways:

1. In the browser by the Less JavaScript library

2. On the server side by language or framework; for example, for Node.js there is the Less module (`https://www.npmjs.com/package/less`)

3. Locally on your machine by command line (installed with npm by running `$ npm install -g less`), or a desktop app such as WinLess (`http://winless.org`), CodeKit (`https://codekitapp.com/index.html`), SimpLess (`https://github.com/Paratron/SimpLESS`)

The browser option (on the fly compilation) is suitable for a development environment but suboptimal for a production environment.

Less Variables

Variables reduce redundancy and allow developers to change values quickly by having them in one canonical place, and we know that in design (and styling) we often have to change values very frequently.

We sometimes have some Less code with the variable marked by the @ sign, such as in `@color`:

```
@color: #4D926F;
#header {
  color: @color;
}
h2 {
  color: @color;
}
```

This code will be compiled to the equivalent in CSS:

```
#header {
  color: #4D926F;
}
h2 {
  color: #4D926F;
}
```

The benefit is that in Less, you need to update the color value in only one place versus two in CSS. This is abstraction at its best.

Less Mix-ins

This section is about mix-ins. They are like functions in JavaScript. The syntax for a mix-in is the same as for creating a class selector. For example, this is a `.border` mix-in:

```
.border {
    border-top: dotted 1px black;
    border-bottom: solid 2px black;
}
```

```
#menu a {
    color: #111;
    .border;
}
.post a {
    color: red;
    .border;
}
```

That converts into this CSS, in which the `.border` is replaced with the actual styles, not the name:

```
.border {
  border-top: dotted 1px black;
  border-bottom: solid 2px black;
}
#menu a {
  color: #111;
  border-top: dotted 1px black;
  border-bottom: solid 2px black;
}
.post a {
  color: red;
  border-top: dotted 1px black;
  border-bottom: solid 2px black;
}
```

Even more useful is to pass a parameter to a mix-in. This enables developers to create even more versatile code. For example, `.rounded-corners` is a mix-in that can change size based on the value of the parameter `radius`:

```less
.rounded-corners (@radius: 5px) {
  border-radius: @radius;
  -webkit-border-radius: @radius;
  -moz-border-radius: @radius;
}

#header {
  .rounded-corners;
}
#footer {
  .rounded-corners(10px);
}
```

That code will compile into this in CSS:

```css
#header {
  border-radius: 5px;
  -webkit-border-radius: 5px;
  -moz-border-radius: 5px;
}
#footer {
  border-radius: 10px;
  -webkit-border-radius: 10px;
  -moz-border-radius: 10px;
}
```

Whether you use mix-ins without parameters or with multiple parameters, they are great at creating abstractions and enabling better code reuse.

Less Operations

Less supports operations. With operations, we can perform math functions on numbers, colors, or variables. This is useful for sizing, colors, and other number-related styles.

Here is an example of an operator in Less where we perform multiplication and addition:

```less
@the-border: 1px;
@base-color: #111;
@red:        #842210;

#header {
  color: @base-color * 3;
  border-left: @the-border;
  border-right: @the-border * 2;
}
#footer {
  color: @base-color + #003300;
  border-color: desaturate(@red, 10%);
}
```

That code compiles in this CSS in which the compiler substituted variables and operations for the results of the expressions:

```less
#header {
  color: #333333;
  border-left: 1px;
  border-right: 2px;
}
#footer {
  color: #114411;
  border-color: #7d2717;
}
```

As you can see, Less dramatically improves the reusability of plain CSS. It's a time saver in large projects, as you can create Less modules and reuse them in multiple apps.

Other important Less features (`http://lesscss.org/#docs`) include the following:

- Pattern matching

- Nested rules Functions

- Namespaces

- Scope

- Comments

- Importing

An Example Using a Third-Party API (OpenWeatherMap) and jQuery

In this section we will look at a Weather app example. It is a standalone example that is not a part of the main Message Board application introduced in this chapter and covered in detail in later chapters.

The goal of the Weather app is to just illustrate the combination of jQuery, JSONP, and REST API technologies. The idea of this weather application is to show you an input field for the city name and buttons for metric and imperial systems (C or F degrees). The first view of the Weather application is shown in Figure 3-1. The view has the input field for the city name and two buttons for metric and imperial forecasts (Figure 3-1).

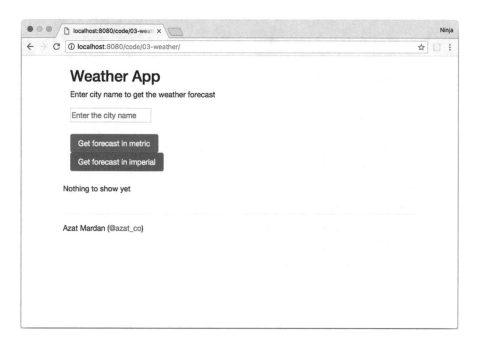

Figure 3-1. *Weather App has a text input field and two buttons for the forecasts*

Once you enter the city name and click one of the buttons, the app will fetch the forecast from OpenWeatherMap. Depending on which button you press, the app will fetch the forecast in metric (C) or imperial (F) degrees. For example, I live in the heart of all the tech innovations, San Francisco, and we use imperial F degrees here, so my result will be similar to the one shown in Figure 3-2. The forecast will be for several days with a 3-hour difference between predictions.

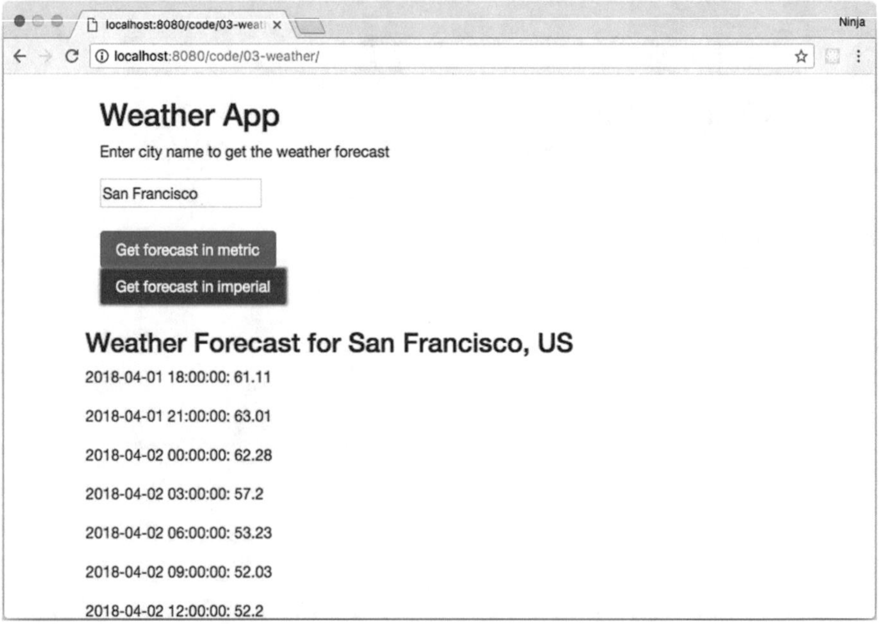

Figure 3-2. *Weather App show the forecast for San Francisco*

Note that this example uses OpenWeatherMap API 2.5. The API requires an authentication (an app ID) for REST calls. You can get the necessary keys at `https://openweathermap.org/appid`. The API documentation is available at `https://openweathermap.org/api`. If you are starting the weather app from the code folder of the repository for this book, then make sure you update the API key, because the key in the provided code may be my key and it may not work in the future.

In this example, we'll use jQuery's `$.ajax()` function. It has the following syntax:

```
const request = $.ajax({
    url: url,
    dataType: 'jsonp',
    data: {q: cityName, appid: appId, units: units},
    jsonpCallback: 'fetchData',
    type: 'GET'
```

```
}).fail(function(error){
  console.error(error)
  alert('Error sending request')
})
```

In the code fragment of the `ajax()` function just shown, we used the following parameters:

- `url` is an endpoint of the API.

- `dataType` is the type of data we expect from the server; for example, `json`, `xml`, `jsonp` (JSON with padding—format for servers that don't support CORS).

- `data` is the data to be sent to the server.

- `jsonpCallback` is a name of the function, in a string format, to be called after the request comes back; by default jQuery will create a name.

- `type` is the HTTP method of the request; for example, `GET`, `POST`.

There is also a chained method `.fail`, which has logic for what to do when the request has an error (i.e., it fails).

For more parameters and examples of the `ajax()` function, go to `http://api.jquery.com/jQuery.ajax`.

To assign our function to a user-triggered event, we need to use the `click()` function from the jQuery library. The syntax is very simple:

```
$('#btn').click(function() {
  ...
}
```

$('#btn') is a jQuery object that points to an HTML element in the DOM with the element ID (id) of btn.

To make sure that all of the elements we want to access and use are in the DOM, we need to enclose all of the DOM manipulation code inside of the following jQuery function:

```
$(document).ready(function(){
  ...
}
```

This is a common mistake with dynamically generated HTML elements. They are not available before they have been created and injected into the DOM.

We must put the event handlers for the buttons in the $(document). ready() callback. Otherwise, the code might try to attach an event listener to a non-existing DOM element. The $(document).ready() callback ensures that the browser rendered all the DOM elements.

```
$(document).ready(function(){
  $('.btn-metric').click(function() {
    prepareData('metric')
  })
  $('.btn-imperial').click(function() {
    prepareData('imperial')
  })
})
```

We use classes instead of IDs, because classes are more flexible (you cannot have more than one ID with the same name). Here's the HTML code for the buttons:

```
<div class="row">
  <div class="span6 offset1">
    <input type="button" class="btn-primary btn
    btn-metric" value="Get forecast in metric"/>
  <div class="span6 offset1">
    <input type="button" class="btn-danger btn
    btn-imperial" value="Get forecast in imperial"/>
  </div>
  <div class="span3">
    <p id="info"></p>
  </div>
</div>
```

The last container with the ID `info` is where we'll put the forecast.

The idea is simple: We have button and event listeners to do something once a user clicks the buttons. The aforementioned buttons call the `prepareData()` method. This is its definition:

```
const openWeatherAppId = 'GET-YOUR-KEY-AT-OPENWEATHERMAP'
const openWeatherUrl = 'http://api.openweathermap.org/
data/2.5/forecast'

const prepareData = function(units) {
  let cityName = $('#city-name').val()
  if (cityName && cityName != ''){
    cityName = cityName.trim()
    getData(openWeatherUrl, cityName, openWeatherAppId,
    units)
  }
  else {
    alert('Please enter the city name')
  }
}
```

The code should be straightforward. We get the value of the city name from the input box (ID `city-name`). Then, we check that the city name is NOT empty, and call `getData()`. This function `getData()` will make the XHR request to the server (Open Weather API). You've already seen an example of the `$.ajax` request. Please note that the callback function is named `fetchData`. This function will be called after the browser gets the response from the OpenWeatherMap API. Needless to say, we must pass the city name, app ID, and units as follows:

```
function getData (url, cityName, appId, units) {
  const request = $.ajax({
    url: url,
    dataType: 'jsonp',
    data: {
      q: cityName,
      appid: appId,
      units: units
    },
    jsonpCallback: 'fetchData',
    type: 'GET'
  }).fail(function(error) {
    console.error(error)
    alert('Error sending request')
  })
}
```

The JSONP fetching function magically (thanks to jQuery) makes cross-domain calls by injecting `<script>` tags and appending the callback function name to the request query string.

At this point, we need to implement `fetchData` and update the view with the forecast. The `console.log` is useful to look up the data structure of the response; that is, where fields are located. The city name and country will be displayed above the forecast to make sure the location found is the same as the one we requested in the input box.

```
function fetchData (forecast) {
    console.log(forecast)
    let html = '',
      cityName = forecast.city.name,
      country = forecast.city.country
```

Now we form the HTML by iterating over the forecast and concatenating the string:

```
html += `<h3> Weather Forecast for ${cityName},
${country}</h3>`
forecast.list.forEach(function(forecastEntry, index, list){
    html += `<p>${forecastEntry.dt_txt}:
    ${forecastEntry.main.temp}</p>`
})
```

Finally, we get a jQuery object for the div with ID `log`, and inject the HTML with the city name and the forecast:

```
$('#log').html(html)
```

In a nutshell, there is a button element that triggers `prepareData()`, which calls `getData()`, in the callback of which is `fetchData()`. If you found that confusing, here's the full code of the `index.html` file:

```
<!DOCTYPE html>
<html lang="en">
<head>
    <link type="text/css" rel="stylesheet" href="css/
    bootstrap.css" />
    <script src="js/jquery.js" type="text/javascript">
    </script>
```

```html
<meta name="viewport" content="width=device-width,
initial-scale=1.0">
<style type="text/css">
    .row {
        padding-top:1.5em;
    }
</style>
<script>
  const openWeatherAppId = 'GET-YOUR-KEY-AT-
  OPENWEATHERMAP'
  const openWeatherUrl = 'http://api.openweathermap.
  org/data/2.5/forecast'

  const prepareData = function(units) {
    // Replace loading image
    let cityName = $('#city-name').val()
    // Make ajax call, callback
    if (cityName && cityName != ''){
      cityName = cityName.trim()
      getData(openWeatherUrl, cityName,
      openWeatherAppId, units)
    }
    else {
      alert('Please enter the city name')
    }
  }

$(document).ready(function(){

  $('.btn-metric').click(function() {
    prepareData('metric')
  })
```

```javascript
$('.btn-imperial').click(function() {
    prepareData('imperial')
  })
})

function getData (url, cityName, appId, units) {
  const request = $.ajax({
    url: url,
    dataType: "jsonp",
    data: {q: cityName, appid: appId, units: units},
    jsonpCallback: "fetchData",
    type: "GET"
  }).fail(function(error){
    console.error(error)
    alert('Error sending request')
  })
}

function fetchData (forecast) {
  console.log(forecast)
  let html = ''
  let cityName = forecast.city.name
  let country = forecast.city.country

  html += `<h3> Weather Forecast for ${cityName},
  ${country}</h3>`
  forecast.list.forEach(function(forecastEntry,
  index, list){
    html += `<p>${forecastEntry.dt_txt}:
    ${forecastEntry.main.temp}</p>`
  })
```

```
    $('#log').html(html)
  }

  </script>
</head>
<body>
  <div class="container">

    <div class="row">
      <div class="span4 offset3">
        <h2>Weather App</h2>
        <p>Enter city name to get the weather
        forecast</p>
      </div>
      <div class="span6 offset1">
        <input class="span4" type="text"
        placeholder="Enter the city name"
          id="city-name" value=""/>
      </div>
    </div>
    <div class="row">
      <div class="span6 offset1">
        <input type="button" class="btn-primary
        btn btn-metric" value="Get forecast in
        metric"/>
      <div class="span6 offset1">
        <input type="button" class="btn-danger
        btn btn-imperial" value="Get forecast in
        imperial"/>
      </div>
    </div>
```

```
<div class="row">
    <div class="span6 offset1">
        <div id="log">Nothing to show yet</div>
    </div>
</div>

<div class="row">
    <hr/>
    <p>Azat Mardan (<a href="http://twitter.com/
    azatmardan">@azatmardan</a>)</p>
</div>

    </div>
</body>
</html>
```

Try launching it and see if it works with or without the local HTTP server (just opening `index.html` in the browser). It should not work without an HTTP server because of its reliance on JSONP technology. You can get `node-static` or `http-server` command-line tools as described in Chapter 2.

The source code is available in the 03-weather folder and on GitHub (`https://github.com/azat-co/fullstack-javascript/tree/master/code/03-weather`).

This example was built with OpenWeatherMap API v2.5 and might not work with later versions. Also, you need the API key called app ID. You can get the necessary keys at `https://openweathermap.org/appid`. If you feel that there must be a working example, please submit your feedback to the GitHub repository for the book's projects (`https://github.com/azat-co/fullstack-javascript`).

jQuery is a good library for getting data from the RESTful servers. Sometimes we are not just reading the data from the servers; we also want to write it. This way the information persists and can be accessed later. Parse will allow you to save your data without friction.

Parse

Parse (`https://parseplatform.org`) is a platform that is a feature-rich backend with convenient API and libraries. One of them is `parse-server` that allows developers to focus on building their client apps (web or mobile) instead of spending time on the backend. Developers can substitute Parse for a database and a server. In other words, with Parse, there's no need to build your own server or to maintain a database!

Parse started as a means to support mobile application development. Nevertheless, with the REST API and the JavaScript SDK, Parse can be used in any web and desktop applications for data storage (and much more), making it ideal for rapid prototyping.

To create a local instance of Parse simply install two npm modules: `parse-server` and `mongodb-runner` using npm:

```
npm i -g parse-server mongodb-runner
```

Then launch the MongoDB database with `mongodb-runner start`. You'll see this message:

```
⌐ Starting a MongoDB deployment to test against...✓
  Downloaded MongoDB 3.6.3
⌐ Starting a MongoDB deployment to test against...
```

That's it. You can create your own backend locally with the next command, which take API key and ID and points to the local DB:

```
parse-server --appId APPLICATION_ID --masterKey MASTER_KEY
--databaseURI mongodb://localhost/test
```

Create your back-end Parse server application. Feel free to use your own values for `appId` and `masterKey`. Copy the Application ID and the master key into the front-end project files, such as `03-parse-sdk/app.js`, because you'll need to use the exact same value on the frontend in order to be able to access your back-end server. In other words, we'll need these keys to access our data collection at Parse.

We'll create a simple application that will save values to the collections using the Parse JavaScript SDK. (A collection is like a table in the traditional SQL/relational database). The final solution is in the `03-parse-sdk` folder. Our application will consist of an `index.html` file and an `app.js` file. Here is the structure of our project folder:

```
/03-parse-sdk
  -index.html
  -app.js
  -jquery.js
  /css
    -boostrap.css
```

The sample is available in the 03-parse-sdk folder on GitHub (`https://github.com/azat-co/fullstack-javascript/tree/master/code/03-parse-sdk`), but you are encouraged to type your own code from scratch. To start, create the `index.html` file:

```
<html lang="en">
<head>
```

Include the minified jQuery library from the local file. You can download it from `https://jquery.com` and save it into the folder. Versions 2, 3 or higher should work fine.

```
<script
  type="text/javascript"
  src=
  "jquery.js">
</script>
```

Include the Parse JavaScript SDK library v1.11.1 from this location `https://unpkg.com/parse@1.11.1/dist/parse.js` or from code for this book (`http://bit.ly/2uEjekR`):

```
<script src="parse-1.11.1.js"></script>
```

Include our `app.js` file and the Bootstrap library (v4 or higher):

```
<script type="text/javascript" src="app.js"></script>
<link type="text/css" rel="stylesheet" href="css/
bootstrap.css" />
</head>
<body>
  <!-- We'll do something here -->
</body>
</html>
```

The `<body>` of the HTML page consists of the `<textarea>` element. We'll use it to enter JSON:

```
<body>
    <div class="container-fluid">
        <div class="row-fluid">
            <div class="col-md-12">
                <div id="content">
                    <div class="row-fluid">
                        <div class="col-md-12">
                            <div class="hero-unit">
                                <h1>Parse JavaScript SDK demo</h1>
                                <textarea cols="60" rows="7">{
  "name": "John",
  "text": "hi"
}</textarea>
```

The indentation of the `<textarea>` looks out of whack because this element preserves white space and we don't want to have it when we process that string into JSON.

After the input area, there's a button that will trigger the saving to Parse:

```
<p><a class="btn btn-primary btn-large
btn-save" >Save object</a></p>
<pre class="log"></pre>
Go to <a href="http://parseplatform.org/"
target="_blank">Parse</a> to check the data.
            </div> *<!-- hero-unit -->*
        </div> *<!-- col-md-12 -->*
      </div> *<!-- row-fluid -->*
    </div> *<!-- content -->*
  </div> *<!-- col-md-12 -->*
 </div> *<!-- row-fluid -->*
</div> *<!-- container-fluid -->*
  </body>
</html>
```

Create the `app.js` file and use the `$(document).ready` function to make sure that the DOM is ready for manipulation:

```
$(document).ready(function() {
```

Change `parseApplicationId` and `parseJavaScriptKey` to values for your own Parse server (you define them when you start the Parse server):

```
const parseApplicationId = 'APPLICATION_ID'
const parseJavaScriptKey = 'MASTER_KEY'
```

Because we've included the Parse JavaScript SDK library, we now have access to the global object `Parse`. We initialize a connection with the keys, and create a reference to a `Test` collection:

```
Parse.initialize(parseApplicationId, parseJavaScriptKey)
Parse.serverURL = 'http://localhost:1337/parse'
```

Next, create the collection object. It's like a model for our data. The name is `Test` but it can be any string value.

```
const Test = Parse.Object.extend('Test')
const test = new Test()
const query = new Parse.Query(Test)
```

The next step is to implement the code to save an object with the keys `name` and `text` to the Parse `Test` collection. We are going to use `test.save()`:

```
test.save(obj, {success, error})
```

But before we can call `save()`, we must get the data from the DOM (browser element `textarea`). The next few statements deal with getting your JSON from the `<textarea>` and parsing it into a normal JavaScript object. The `try/catch` is crucial because the JSON structure is very rigid. You cannot have any extra symbols. Each time there's a syntax error, it will break the entire app. Therefore, we need to account for erroneous syntax:

```
try {
  const data = JSON.parse($('textarea').val())
} catch (e) {
  alert('Invalid JSON')
}
```

Conveniently, the `save()` method accepts the callback parameters `success` and `error` just like the `jQuery.ajax()` function. To get a confirmation, we'll just have to look at the `log` container (`<pre class="log"></pre>`) on the page:

```
test.save(data, {
  success: (result) => {
      console.log('Parse.com object is saved: ', result)
      $('.log').html(JSON.stringify(result, null, 2))
  },
  error: (error) => {
    console.log(`Error! Parse.com object is not saved:
    ${error}`)
  }
})
```

It's important to know why we failed to save an object. That's why there's an error callback.

We will also implement a method to get all objects from `Test`. We will use `query.find()`. Just so you don't have to click the GitHub link (or type it from the book) to look up the full source code of the `app.js` file, I provide it here:

```
const parseAppID = 'APPLICATION_ID'
const parseRestKey = 'MASTER_KEY'
const apiBase = `http://localhost:1337/parse`
$(document).ready(function(){
  getMessages()
  $('#send').click(function(){
    const $sendButton = $(this)
    $sendButton.html('<img src="img/spinner.gif"
    width="20"/>')
```

```javascript
    const username = $('input[name=username]').val()
    const message = $('input[name=message]').val()
    $.ajax({
      url: `${apiBase}/classes/MessageBoard`,
      headers: {
        'X-Parse-Application-Id': parseAppID,
        'X-Parse-REST-API-Key': parseRestKey
      },
      contentType: 'application/json',
      dataType: 'json',
      processData: false,
      data: JSON.stringify({
        'username': username,
        'message': message
      }),
      type: 'POST',
      success: function() {
        console.log('sent')
        getMessages()
        $sendButton.html('SEND')
      },
      error: function() {
        console.log('error')
        $sendButton.html('SEND')
      }
    })
  })
})

function getMessages() {
  $.ajax({
    url: `${apiBase}/classes/MessageBoard?limit=1000`,
```

```
    headers: {
      'X-Parse-Application-Id': parseAppID,
      'X-Parse-REST-API-Key': parseRestKey
    },
    contentType: 'application/json',
    dataType: 'json',
    type: 'GET',
    success: (data) => {
      console.log('get')
      updateView(data)
    },
    error: () => {
      console.log('error')
    }
  })
}

function updateView(messages) {
  // messages.results = messages.results.reverse()
  const table = $('.table tbody')
  table.html(``)
  $.each(messages.results, (index, value) => {
    const trEl = (`<tr><td>
      ${value.username}
      </td><td>
      ${value.message}
      </td></tr>`)
    table.append(trEl)
  })
  console.log(messages)
}
```

To run the app, start your local web server at the project folder and navigate to the address (e.g., http://localhost:8080) in your browser. Or you can start the static web server from my book repository. The difference is that you'll have to provide the path `code/03-parse-sdk` if you start from the book repository folder (root). If you start from the project folder then you do not provide the path because the `index.html` file is right in the project folder. Note that if you get a 401 Unauthorized error from Parse, that's probably because you have the wrong API key. Make sure you use the same key in your JavaScript as you used when you started the `parse-server` from the command line. Of course, if you haven't started your `parse-serve`, do so now because you cannot connect to a server if it's not running.

If everything was done properly, you should be able to see the `Test` collection in Parse's Data Browser populated with values "John" and "hi" (Figure 3-3). Also, you should see the proper message with the newly created ID. Parse automatically creates object IDs and timestamps, which will be very useful in our Message Board application.

Figure 3-3. *Clicking the "Save object" button will send the object to the backend, which will save it to the database*

If you press on the "Get objects" green button, then you'll get all the objects which are stored in the database. How to confirm that this data is actually stored in the database and won't disappear when we close the browser? Simply close the browser and open it again. If you're still not convinced, use Mongo shell/REPL (`mongo`), my web-based tool `mongoui` (`npm i -g mongoui`) or desktop app Compass (Figure 3-4) to go to the local MongoDB database instance and the `Test` collection. There will be the data just sitting and looking at you.

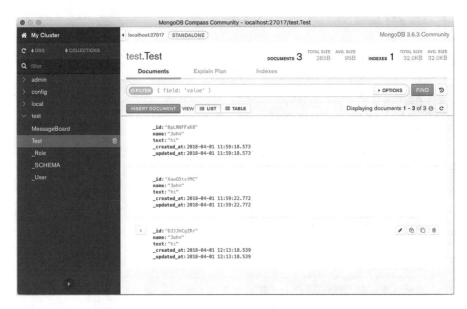

Figure 3-4. *Compass shows in MongoDB the data which was sent from the browser*

Parse also has thorough instructions for the various parts of the platform, including its server and client libraries: `http://docs.parseplatform.org`. You can deploy `parse-server` into the cloud or your own data center. Parse supports containers too.

With Parse, which is a one command (`parse-server`), we call browser JavaScript methods and wheyeee, we work with the database straight from the browser!

Let's move on to the Message Board app.

Message Board with Parse Overview

The Message Board will consist of an input field, a list of messages, and a "SEND" button (see Figure 3-5). We need to display a list of existing messages and be able to submit new messages. We'll use Parse as a backend for now, and later switch to Node.js with MongoDB.

Figure 3-5. *The messages and the new message form with the "SEND" button*

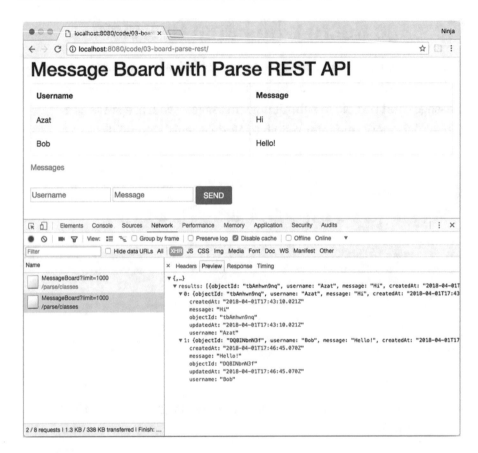

Figure 3-6. *The GET XHR calls fetches all the first 1000 messages form the backend*

You can get a free copy of the parse-server from npm. It's just an open source library which you can run anywhere. Unlike the previous example in which we used the Parse SDK, in this example we will be making our own AJAX/XHR calls to the backend. This will prepare us for switching to our own backend.

After installing Parse server (`npm i -g parse-server`), launch it with the app ID and the key. Write them down in invisible ink on a newspaper. You will need them later. There are a few ways to use Parse:

- *REST API*: We're going to use this approach with the jQuery example.

- *JavaScript SDK*: We just used this approach in our preceding `Test` example, and we'll use it in the Backbone.js example later.

Using the REST API is a more generic approach. Parse provides endpoints that we can request with the `$.ajax()` method from the jQuery library. The description of available URLs and methods can be found at `http://docs.parseplatform.org`.

Message Board with Parse: REST API and jQuery Version

The full code is available in the 03-board-parse-rest (`https://github.com/azat-co/fullstack-javascript/tree/master/code/03-board-parse-rest`) folder, but I encourage you to try to write your own application first.

We'll use Parse's REST API and jQuery. Parse supports different origin domain AJAX calls, so we won't need JSONP.

When you decide to deploy your back-end application, which will act as a substitute for Parse, on a different domain you'll need to use either JSONP on the front end or custom CORS headers on a backend. This topic is covered later in the book.

Right now the structure of the application should look like this:

```
index.html
  css/bootstrap.min.css
  css/style.css
  js/app.js
  js/jquery.js
  img/spinner.gif
```

Let's create a visual representation for the Message Board app. We just want to display a list of messages with names of users in chronological order. Therefore, a table will do just fine, and we can dynamically create `<tr>` elements and keep inserting them as we get new messages.

Create a simple HTML file `index.html` with the following content:

- Inclusion of JS and CSS files

- Responsive structure with Bootstrap

- A table of messages

- A form for new messages

Let's start with the `<head>` and dependencies. We'll include CDN jQuery, local `app.js`, local minified Bootstrap, and custom stylesheet `style.css`:

```
<!DOCTYPE html>
<html lang="en">
  <head>
    <script src="js/jquery.js" type="text/javascript"
    language="javascript" ></script>
    <script src="js/app.js" type="text/javascript"
    language="javascript" ></script>
    <link href="css/bootstrap.min.css" type="text/css"
    rel="stylesheet" />
```

110

```html
<link href="css/style.css" type="text/css"
rel="stylesheet" />
<meta name="viewport" content="width=device-width,
initial-scale=1">
</head>
```

The `<body>` element will have typical Bootstrap scaffolding elements defined by classes `container-fluid` and `row-fluid`:

```html
<body>
  <div class="container-fluid">
    <div class="row-fluid">
      <h1>Message Board with Parse REST API</h1>
```

The table of messages is empty, because we'll populate it programmatically from within the JS code:

```html
<table class="table table-bordered table-striped">
  <caption>Messages</caption>
  <thead>
    <tr>
      <th>
        Username
      </th>
      <th>
        Message
      </th>
    </tr>
  </thead>
  <tbody>
    <tr>
      <td colspan="2"><img src="img/spinner.gif"
      width="20"/></td>
    </tr>
```

```
      </tbody>
    </table>
  </div>
```

Another row and here is our new message form in which the Send button uses Bootstrap classes `btn` and `btn-primary`:

```
<div class="row-fluid">
  <form id="new-user">
    <input type="text" name="username"
      placeholder="Username" />
    <input type="text" name="message"
      placeholder="Message" />
    <a id="send" class="btn btn-primary">SEND</a>
  </form>
</div>
</div>
</body>
</html>
```

The table will contain our messages and the form will provide input for new messages. Now we are going to write three main functions:

1. `getMessages()`: The function to get the messages

2. `updateView()`: The function to render the list of messages

3. `$('#send').click(...)`: The function that triggers sending a new message

To keep things simple, we'll put all of the logic in one file `app.js`. Of course, it is a good idea to separate code base on the functionality when your project grows larger.

Replace these values with your own, and be careful to use the REST API key (not the JavaScript SDK key from the previous example):

```
const parseAppID = 'APPLICATION_ID'
const parseRestKey = 'MASTER_KEY'
const apiBase = `http://localhost:1337/parse`
```

Let's start with `document.ready`. It will have the logic for fetching messages, and define the Send button's `click` event:

```
$(document).ready(function(){
    getMessages()
    $('#send').click(function(){
```

Let's save the button object:

```
const $sendButton = $(this)
```

We should show a spinner image ("Loading...") on the button because the request might take some time and we want users to see that our app is working, not just freezing for no apparent reason.

```
$sendButton.html('<img src="img/spinner.gif"
width="20"/>')
const username = $('input[name=username]').val()
const message = $('input[name=message]').val()
```

When we submit a new message (a POST request), we make the HTTP call with the `jQuery.ajax` function. A full list of parameters for the `ajax` function is available at `http://api.jquery.com/jQuery.ajax`. The most important ones are URL, headers, and type parameters.

```
$.ajax({
    url: `${apiBase}/classes/MessageBoard`,
    headers: {
        'X-Parse-Application-Id': parseAppID,
        'X-Parse-REST-API-Key': parseRestKey
    },
    contentType: 'application/json',
```

The type of the data is JSON:

```
    dataType: 'json',
    processData: false,
    data: JSON.stringify({
        'username': username,
        'message': message
    }),
    type: 'POST',
    success: function() {
        console.log('sent')
```

Assuming that our POST request to Parse saved the new message (`success`), we now want to get the updated list of messages that will include our message, and replace the spinner image with text as it was before someone clicked the button:

```
        getMessages()
        $sendButton.html('SEND')
    },
    error: function() {
        console.log('error')
        $sendButton.html('SEND')
    }
})
```

To summarize, clicking the Send button will send a POST request to the Parse REST API and then, on successful response, get messages calling the getMessages() function.

The getMessages() method to fetch messages from our remote REST API server also uses the jQuery.ajax function. The URL has the name of the collection (MessageBoard) and a query string parameter that sets the limit at 1,000:

```
function getMessages() {
  $.ajax({
    url: `${apiBase}/classes/MessageBoard?limit=1000`,
```

We need to pass the keys in a header:

```
headers: {
  'X-Parse-Application-Id': parseAppID,
  'X-Parse-REST-API-Key': parseRestKey
},
contentType: 'application/json',
dataType: 'json',
type: 'GET',
```

If the request is completed successfully (status 200/ok or similar), we call the updateView() function:

```
    success: (data) => {
      console.log('get')
      updateView(data)
    },
    error: () => {
      console.log('error')
    }
  })
}
```

Then, on successful response, it will call the `updateView()` function, which clears the table `tbody` and iterates through results of the response using the `$.each()` jQuery function (`http://api.jquery.com/jQuery.each`).

This function is rendering the list of messages that we get from the server:

```
function updateView(messages) {
```

We use the jQuery selector `.table tbody` to create an object referencing that element. Then we clean all the `innerHTML` of that element:

```
const table=$('.table tbody')
table.html('')
```

We use the `jQuery.each()` function to iterate through every message. The following code creates HTML elements (and the jQuery object of those elements) programmatically:

```
$.each(messages.results, (index, value) => {
  const trEl = (`<tr><td>
    ${value.username}
      </td><td>
      ${value.message}
      </td></tr>`)
  table.append(trEl)
})
```

In a sense `trEl` is a string with HTML for each message or row in the message board. The next line appends (injects after) the table's `tbody` element our row.

Here is another way to dynamically create an HTML element (e.g., `div`) using jQuery:

```
$('<div>')
```

For your reference, here is the entire `app.js`:

```js
const parseAppID = 'APPLICATION_ID'
const parseRestKey = 'MASTER_KEY'
const apiBase = `http://localhost:1337/parse`

$(document).ready(function(){
  getMessages()
  $('#send').click(function(){
    const $sendButton = $(this)
    $sendButton.html('<img src="img/spinner.gif"
    width="20"/>')
    const username = $('input[name=username]').val()
    const message = $('input[name=message]').val()
    $.ajax({
      url: `${apiBase}/classes/MessageBoard`,
      headers: {
        'X-Parse-Application-Id': parseAppID,
        'X-Parse-REST-API-Key': parseRestKey
      },
      contentType: 'application/json',
      dataType: 'json',
      processData: false,
      data: JSON.stringify({
        'username': username,
        'message': message
      }),
      type: 'POST',
      success: function() {
        console.log('sent')
        getMessages()
        $sendButton.html('SEND')
      },
```

```
      error: function() {
        console.log('error')
        $sendButton.html('SEND')
      }
    })
  })
})

function getMessages() {
  $.ajax({
    url: `${apiBase}/classes/MessageBoard?limit=1000`,
    headers: {
      'X-Parse-Application-Id': parseAppID,
      'X-Parse-REST-API-Key': parseRestKey
    },
    contentType: 'application/json',
    dataType: 'json',
    type: 'GET',
    success: (data) => {
      console.log('get')
      updateView(data)
    },
    error: () => {
      console.log('error')
    }
  })
}

function updateView(messages) {
  const table = $('.table tbody')
  table.html("")
  $.each(messages.results, (index, value) => {
    const trEl = (`<tr><td>
```

```
${value.username}
  </td><td>
  ${value.message}
  </td></tr>`)
table.append(trEl)
})
console.log(messages)
}
```

Try running the code with your local HTTP server. You should see the messages (obviously, there should be no messages for the very first time) and by clicking the button be able to post new ones.

This is fine if all you need to do is develop the app on your local machine, but what about deploying it to the cloud? To do that, we'll need to apply version control with Git first.

Pushing to GitHub

To create a GitHub repository, go to `https://github.com`, log in, and create a new repository. There will be an SSH address; copy it. In your terminal window, navigate to the project folder that you would like to push to GitHub.

1. Create a local Git and `.git` folder in the root of the project folder:

    ```
    $ git init
    ```

2. Add all of the files to the repository and start tracking them:

    ```
    $ git add .
    ```

3. Make the first commit:

```
$ git commit -am "initial commit"
```

4. Add the GitHub remote destination:

```
$ git remote add your-github-repo-ssh-url
```

It might look something like this:

```
$ git remote add origin git@github.
com:azat-co/simple-message-board.git
```

5. Now everything should be set to push your local Git repository to the remote destination on GitHub with the following command:

```
$ git push origin master
```

6. You should be able to see your files at under your account and repository `https://github.com/YOUR_USERNAME/YOUR_REPO_NAME`

Later, when you make changes to the file, there is no need to repeat all of these steps. Just execute:

```
$ git add .
$ git commit -am "some message"
$ git push origin master
```

If there are no new untracked files you want to start tracking, use this:

```
$ git commit -am "some message"
$ git push origin master
```

To include changes from individual files, run:

```
$ git commit filename -m "some message"
$ git push origin master
```

To remove a file from the Git repository, use:

```
$ git rm filename
```

For more Git commands, see:

```
$ git --help
```

Deploying applications with Microsoft Azure or Heroku is as simple as pushing code and files to GitHub. The last three steps (4–6) would be substituted with a different remote destination (URL) and a different alias.

Deployment to Microsoft Azure

You should be able to deploy to Microsoft Azure with Git using this procedure.

1. Go to the Microsoft Azure Portal at `https://portal.azure.com`, log in with your Live ID, and create a web site if you haven't done so already. Enable Set Up Git Publishing by providing a user name and password (they should be different from your Live ID credentials). Copy your URL somewhere.

2. Create a local Git repository in the project folder that you would like to publish or deploy:

   ```
   $ git init
   ```

3. Add all of the files to the repository and start tracking them:

   ```
   $ git add .
   ```

4. Make the first commit:

   ```
   $ git commit -am "initial commit"
   ```

5. Add Microsoft Azure as a remote Git repository destination:

```
$ git remote add azure your-url-for-
remote-repository
```

In my case, this command looked like this:

```
$ git remote add
> azure https://azatazure@azat.scm.
azurewebsites.net/azat.git
```

6. Push your local Git repository to the remote Microsoft Azure repository, which will deploy the files and application:

```
$ git push azure master
```

As with GitHub, there is no need to repeat the first few steps when you have updated the files later, as we already should have a local Git repository in the form of a `.git` folder in the root of the project folder.

Deployment of Weather App to Heroku

The only major difference from deploying to Azure is that Heroku uses Cedar Stack, which doesn't support static projects, including plain HTML applications like our Weather app. In the folder of the project that you would like to publish or deploy to Heroku, create a file `index.php` on the same level as `index.html`, with the following content:

```
<?php echo file_get_contents('index.html'); ?>
```

For your convenience, the `index.php` file is already included in `weather`.

There is an even simpler way to publish static files on Heroku with Cedar Stack. To make Cedar Stack work with your static files, all you need to do is to type and execute the following commands in your project folder:

```
$ touch index.php
$ echo 'php_flag engine off' > .htaccess
```

Alternatively, you could use the Ruby Bamboo stack. In this case, you would need the following structure:

```
-project folder
  -config.ru
  /public
    -index.html
    -/css
    app.js
    ...
```

The path in `index.html` to CSS and other assets should be relative; for example, `css/style.css`. The `config.ru` file should contain the following code:

```ruby
use Rack::Static,
  :urls => ["/stylesheets", "/images"],
  :root => "public"

run lambda { |env|
  [
    200,
    {
      'Content-Type' => 'text/html',
      'Cache-Control' => 'public, max-age=86400'
    },
    File.open('public/index.html', File::RDONLY)
  ]
}
```

123

For more details, you can refer to `https://devcenter.heroku.com/articles/static-sites-ruby`. Once you have all of the support files for Cedar Stack or Bamboo, follow these steps:

1. Create a local Git repository and `.git` folder if you haven't done so already:

   ```
   $ git init
   ```

2. Add files:

   ```
   $ git add .
   ```

3. Commit files and changes:

   ```
   $ git commit -m "my first commit"
   ```

4. Create the Heroku Cedar Stack application and add the remote destination:

   ```
   $ heroku create
   ```

   If everything went well, it should tell you that the remote destination has been added and the app has been created, and give you the app name.

5. To look up the remote destination type and execute (*optional*):

   ```
   $ git remote show
   ```

6. Deploy the code to Heroku with:

   ```
   $ git push heroku master
   ```

   Terminal logs should tell you whether or not the deployment went smoothly.

7.   To open the app in your default browser, type:

```
$ heroku open
```

or just go to the URL of your app, something like

```
http://yourappname-NNNN.herokuapp.com
```

8.   To look at the Heroku logs for this app, type:

```
$ heroku logs
```

To update the app with the new code, repeat the following steps only:

```
$ git add -A
$ git commit -m "commit for deploy to heroku"
$ git push -f heroku
```

You'll be assigned a new application URL each time you create a new Heroku app with the command: `$ heroku create`.

Updating and Deleting Messages

In accordance with the REST API, an update on an object is performed via the PUT method and a delete is performed with the DELETE method. Both of them can easily be performed with the same `jQuery.ajax()` function that we've used for GET and POST, as long as we provide an ID of an object on which we want to execute an operation. The ID can be stored in the DOM. Try it yourself. Replace the method `type` and add ID to the URL such as:

```
$.ajax({
  type: 'PUT', // new method
  url: `${apiBase}/classes/MessageBoard/${id}`,
  // ID in the URL
```

```
headers: {
  'X-Parse-Application-Id': parseAppID,
  'X-Parse-REST-API-Key': parseRestKey
},
contentType: 'application/json',
dataType: 'json',
processData: false,
data: JSON.stringify({
  'username': username,
  'message': message
}),
success: function() {
  console.log('sent')
  getMessages()
  $sendButton.html('SEND')
},
error: function() {
  console.log('error')
  $sendButton.html('SEND')
}
})
```

Summary

This chapter was a handful. Hopefully you got some helpful ideas about JSON, AJAX, and cross-domain calls. Remember, when accessing servers you'll need to make sure they support CORS or JSONP.

We've covered some of the meatiest Less features and worked with Parse to persist the data. We also deployed our app to the cloud using the Git version system.

CHAPTER 4

Intro to Backbone.js

Code is not an asset. It's a liability. The more you write, the more you'll have to maintain later.

—Unknown

This chapter will demonstrate:

- Setting up a Backbone.js app from scratch and installing dependencies
- Working with Backbone.js collections
- Backbone.js event binding
- Backbone.js views and subviews with Underscore.js
- Refactoring Backbone.js code
- AMD and Require.js for Backbone.js development
- Require.js for Backbone.js production
- A simple Backbone.js starter kit

Backbone.js has been around for a while so it's very mature and can be trusted to be used in serious front- end development projects. This framework is decidedly minimalistic and un-opinionated. You can use Backbone.js with a lot of other libraries and modules. I think of Backbone. js as the foundation to build a custom framework that will be tightly suited to your particular use case.

© Azat Mardan 2018
A. Mardan, *Full Stack JavaScript*, https://doi.org/10.1007/978-1-4842-3718-2_4

Some people are turned off by the fact that Backbone.js is un-opinionated and minimalistic. They prefer frameworks that do more for them and enforce a particular way of doing things (e.g., the Angular Style Guide, at `https://github.com/johnpapa/angular-styleguide`). This is totally fine with me, and you can pursue the study of a more complex front-end framework. They all fit nicely into the Node.js stack and the ecosystem. For the purpose of this book, Backbone.js is ideal because it provides some much needed sanity to the plain non-framework jQuery code, and at the same time it doesn't have a steep learning curve. All you need to know is a few classes and methods, which we cover in this book. Everything else is JavaScript, not a domain- specific language.

Setting Up a Backbone.js App from Scratch

We're going to build a typical starter Hello World application using Backbone.js and Model-View-Controller (MVC) architecture. It might sound like overkill in the beginning, but as we go along we'll add more and more complexity, including models, subviews, and collections.

Full source code for the Hello World app is available under code/04-backbone/hello-world and on GitHub at `http://bit.ly/2LgXOVp`.

Backbone.js Dependencies

Download the following libraries:

- jQuery development source file: `http://code.jquery.com`

- Underscore.js development source file: `http://underscorejs.org/underscore.js`

- Backbone.js development source file: `http://backbonejs.org/backbone.js`

Obviously by the time this book is in print, these versions won't be the most recent. I recommend sticking with the versions in this book, because that's what I used to test all the examples and projects. Using different, newer versions might cause some unexpected conflicts.

Create an `index.html` file, and include these frameworks in this file like this:

```
<!DOCTYPE>
<html>
<head>
  <script src="jquery.js"></script>
  <script src="underscore.js"></script>
  <script src="backbone.js"></script>

  <script>
    // TODO write some awesome JS code!
  </script>

</head>
<body>
</body>
</html>
```

We can also put `<script>` tags right before the `</body>` tag at the end of the file. This will change the order in which scripts and the rest of the HTML is loaded, and affect performance in large files.

Let's define an empty Backbone.js router object `router` inside of a `<script>` tag using the `extend()`:

```
// ...
const router = Backbone.Router.extend({
})
// ...
```

For now, to keep it simple (KISS-keep it stupid simple), we'll be putting all of our JavaScript code right into the `index.html` file. This is not a good idea for real development or production code, so we'll refactor it later.

Next, set up a special `routes` property inside of an `extend` call:

```
const router = Backbone.Router.extend({
  routes: {
  }
})
```

The Backbone.js `routes` property needs to be in the following format:

```
'path/:param':'action'
```

This will result in the `filename#path/param` URL triggering a function named `action` (defined in the `Router` object). For now, we'll add a single `home` route:

```
const router = Backbone.Router.extend({
  routes: {
    '': 'home'
  }
})
```

This is good, but now we need to add a `home` function:

```
const router = Backbone.Router.extend({
  routes: {
    '': 'home'
  },
  home: function() {
    // TODO render HTML
  }
})
```

We'll come back to the `home` function later to add more logic for creating and rendering of a view (instance of a `View` class in Backbone). Right now we should define our `homeView`:

```
const homeView = Backbone.View.extend({
})
```

It looks familiar, right? Backbone.js uses similar syntax for all of its components: the `extend` function and a JSON object as a parameter to it.

There are a multiple ways to proceed from now on, but the best practice is to use the `el` and `template` properties, which are special in Backbone.js:

```
const homeView = Backbone.View.extend({
  el: 'body',
  template: _.template('Hello World')
})
```

The property `el` is just a string that holds the jQuery selector (you can use class name with . and id name with #). The `template` property has been assigned an `Underscore.js` function `template` with just a plain text 'Hello World'.

To render our `homeView` we use `this.$el`, which is a compiled jQuery object referencing an element in an `el` property, and the jQuery `.html()` function to replace HTML with the `this.template()` value. Here is what the full code for our Backbone.js View looks like:

```
const homeView = Backbone.View.extend({
  el: 'body',
  template: _.template('Hello World'),
  render: function() {
    this.$el.html(this.template({}))
  }
})
```

Now, if we go back to the `router` we can add these two lines to the `home` function:

```
const router = Backbone.Router.extend({
  routes: {
    '': 'home'
  },
  initialize: function() {
  },
  home: function() {
    this.homeView = new homeView
    this.homeView.render()
  }
})
```

The first line creates the `homeView` object and assigns it to the `homeView` property of the router object `router`. The second line will call the `render()` method in the `homeView` object, triggering the "Hello World" output.

Finally, to start a Backbone app, we call `new Router` inside of a document-ready wrapper to make sure that the file's DOM is fully loaded:

```
let app
$(document).ready(function(){
  app = new router
  Backbone.history.start()
})
```

This time, I won't list the full source code of the `index.html` file because it's rather simple.

Open `index.html` in the browser to see if it works; that is, the "Hello World" message should be on the page.

Working with Backbone.js Collections

The full source code of this example is under 04-backbone/collections. It's built on top of the "Hello World" example from the "Setting Up a Backbone.js App from Scratch" exercise, which is available for download at GitHub (`https://github.com/azat-co/fullstack-javascript/tree/master/code/04-backbone/collections`).

We should add some data to play around with, and to hydrate our views. To do this, add this right after the `<script>` tag and before the other code:

```
const appleData = [
  {
    name: 'fuji',
    url: 'img/fuji.jpg'
  },
  {
    name: 'gala',
    url: 'img/gala.jpg'
  }
]
```

This is our apple *database,* or to be more correct, our REST API endpoint substitute, which provides us with names and image URLs of the apples (data models). Note that this mock data set can be easily substituted by assigning REST API endpoints of your backend to `url` properties in Backbone.js collections, models, or both, and calling the `fetch()` method on them.

Now to make the user experience a little bit better, we can add a new route to the `routes` object in the Backbone `route`:

```
// ...
routes: {
  '': 'home',
  'apples/:appleName': 'loadApple'
},
// ...
```

This will allow users to go to `index.html#apples/SOMENAME` and expect to see some information about an apple. This information will be fetched and rendered by the `loadApple` function in the Backbone router definition:

```
loadApple: function(appleName) {
  this.appleView.render(appleName)
}
```

Have you noticed an `appleName` variable? It's exactly the same name as the one that we've used in `route`. This is how we can access query string parameters (e.g., `?param=value&q=search`) in Backbone.js.

Now we'll need to refactor some more code to create a Backbone collection, populate it with data in our `appleData` variable, and pass the collection to `homeView` and `appleView`. Conveniently enough, we do it all in the router constructor method `initialize`:

```
initialize: function(){
  const apples = new Apples()
  apples.reset(appleData)
  this.homeView = new homeView({collection: apples})
  this.appleView = new appleView({collection: apples})
},
```

At this point, we're pretty much done with the `Router` class and it should look like this:

```
const router = Backbone.Router.extend({
  routes: {
    '': 'home',
    'apples/:appleName': 'loadApple'
  },
  initialize: function(){
    const apples = new Apples()
    apples.reset(appleData)
    this.homeView = new homeView({collection: apples})
    this.appleView = new appleView({collection: apples})
  },
  home: function(){
    this.homeView.render()
  },
  loadApple: function(appleName){
    this.appleView.render(appleName)
  }
})
```

Let's modify our `homeView` a bit to see the whole database:

```
const homeView = Backbone.View.extend({
  el: 'body',
  template: _.template('Apple data: <%= data %>'),
  render: function(){
    this.$el.html(this.template({data: JSON.
    stringify(this.collection.models)}))
  }
  // TODO subviews
})
```

For now, we just output the string representation of the JSON object in the browser. This is not user-friendly at all, but later we'll improve it by using a list and subviews.

Our apple Backbone `Collection` `Apples` is very clean and simple:

```
const Apples = Backbone.Collection.extend({
})
```

Backbone automatically creates models inside of a collection when we use the `fetch()` or `reset()` functions from its API. I find using these functions to be very useful.

`appleView` is not any more complex; it has only two properties: `template` and `render`. In a template, we want to display `figure`, `img`, and `figcaption` tags with specific values. The Underscore.js template engine is handy at this task:

```
const appleView = Backbone.View.extend({
  template: _.template(
    '<figure>\
        <img src="<%= attributes.url %>"/>\
        <figcaption><%= attributes.name %></figcaption>\
    </figure>'),
  // ...
})
```

To make a JavaScript string that has HTML tags in it more readable, we can use the backslash line breaker escape (\) symbol, or close strings and concatenate them with a plus sign (+). This is an example of `appleView` introduced earlier, which is refactored using the latter approach:

```
const appleView = Backbone.View.extend({
  template: _.template(
    '<figure>'+
      +'<img src="<%= attributes.url %>"/>'+
      +'<figcaption><%= attributes.name %></figcaption>'+
      +'</figure>'),
// ...
})
```

Please note the <%= and %> symbols; they are the instructions for Undescore.js to print values in properties url and name of the attributes object.

Finally, we're adding the render function to the appleView class.

```
render: function(appleName) {
```

To get the list of apples filtered by name, there's a where method on the Collection class. We just need the very first item in that array, and because arrays in JavaScript are zero-based (they start with a 0 rather than 1 index), the syntax to get the apple model by name is this:

```
const appleModel = this.collection.where({name:
appleName})[0]
```

Once we have our model, all we need to do is to pass the model to the template (also called hydrating templates). The result is some HTML that we inject into the <body>:

```
  const appleHtml = this.template(appleModel)
  $('body').html(appleHtml)
}
```

So we find a model within the collection via the `where()` method and use `[]` to pick the first element. Right now, the `render` function is responsible for both loading the data and rendering it. Later we'll refactor the function to separate these two functionalities into different methods.

For your convenience, here's the whole app, which is in the `04-backbone/collections/index.html` file and on GitHub at `http://bit.ly/2Lee1L9`:

```
<!DOCTYPE>
<html>
<head>
  <script src="jquery.js"></script>
  <script src="underscore.js"></script>
  <script src="backbone.js"></script>

  <script>
    const appleData = [
      {
        name: 'fuji',
        url: 'img/fuji.jpg'
      },
      {
        name: 'gala',
        url: 'img/gala.jpg'
      }
    ]
    let app
    const router = Backbone.Router.extend({
      routes: {
        '': 'home',
        'apples/:appleName': 'loadApple'
      },
```

```
  initialize: function(){
    const apples = new Apples()
    apples.reset(appleData)
    this.homeView = new homeView({collection: apples})
    this.appleView = new appleView({collection: apples})
  },
  home: function() {
    this.homeView.render()
  },
  loadApple: function(appleName) {
    this.appleView.render(appleName)
  }
})

const homeView = Backbone.View.extend({
  el: 'body',
  template: _.template('Apple data: <%= data %>'),
  render: function() {
    this.$el.html(this.template({data: JSON.
    stringify(this.collection.models)}))
  }
})

const Apples = Backbone.Collection.extend({

})
const appleView = Backbone.View.extend({
  template: _.template('<figure>\
                        <img src="<%= attributes.
                        url%>"/>\
                        <figcaption><%= attributes.
                        name %></figcaption>\
                   </figure>'),
```

```
    render: function(appleName) {
      const appleModel = this.collection.where({name:
      appleName})[0]
      const appleHtml = this.template(appleModel)
      $('body').html(appleHtml)
    }
  })
  $(document).ready(function() {
    app = new router
    Backbone.history.start()
  })

  </script>
</head>
<body>
  <div></div>
</body>
</html>
```

Open the `collections/index.html` file in your browser. You should see the data from our database:

```
Apple data: [{"name":"fuji","url":"img/fuji.jpg"},
{"name":"gala","url":"img/gala.jpg"}]
```

Now let's go to `collections/index.html#apples/fuji` or `collections/index.html#apples/gala` in your browser. We expect to see an image with a caption. It's a detailed view of an item, which in this case is an apple. Nice work!

Backbone.js Event Binding

In real life, getting data does not happen instantaneously, so let's refactor our code to simulate it. For a better user experience (UX), we'll also have to show a loading icon (a spinner or AJAX loader) to users to notify them that the information is being loaded.

It's a good thing that we have event binding in Backbone. Without it, we would have to pass a function that renders HTML as a callback to the data loading function, to make sure that the rendering function is not executed before we have the actual data to display.

Therefore, when a user goes to detailed view (`apples/:id`) we only call the function that loads the data. Then, with the proper event listeners, our view will automagically (this is not a typo) update itself when there is new data (or on a data change; Backbone.js supports multiple and even custom events).

For your information, if you don't feel like typing out the code (which I recommend), it's in the `code/04-backbone/binding/index.html` file and on GitHub at `http://bit.ly/2LhBNpx`.

Let's change the code in the router:

```
// ...
  loadApple: function(appleName){
    this.appleView.loadApple(appleName)
  }
// ...
```

Everything else remains the same until we get to the `appleView` class. We'll need to add a constructor or an `initialize` method, which is a special word or property in the Backbone.js framework. It's called each time we create an instance of an object, such as `const someObj = new SomeObject()`. We can also pass extra parameters to the `initialize` function, as we did with our views (we passed an object with the key `collection` and the value of `apples` Backbone Collection).

Read more on Backbone.js constructors at `http://backbonejs.org/#View-constructor`.

```
// ...
const appleView = Backbone.View.extend({
  initialize: function(){
    // TODO: create and setup model (aka an apple)
  },
// ...
```

We have our `initialize` function; now we need to create a model that will represent a single apple and set up proper event listeners on the model. We'll use two types of events, `change` and a custom event called `spinner`. To do that, we are going to use the `on()` function, which takes these properties: `on(event, actions, context)`. You can read more about it at `http://backbonejs.org/#Events-on`.

```
// ...
const appleView = Backbone.View.extend({
  initialize: function(){
    this.model = new (Backbone.Model.extend({}))
    this.model.bind('change', this.render, this)
    this.bind('spinner', this.showSpinner, this)
  },
  // ...
})
// ...
```

The preceding code basically boils down to two simple things:

1. Call the `render()` function of the `appleView` object when the model has changed.

2. Call the `showSpinner()` method of the `appleView` object when event `spinner` has been fired.

So far, so good, right? But what about the spinner, a GIF icon? Let's create a new property in `appleView`:

```
// ...
  templateSpinner: '<img src="img/spinner.gif"
  width="30"/>',
// ...
```

Remember the `loadApple` call in the router? This is how we can implement the function in `appleView`:

```
...
loadApple: function (appleName)  {
```

To show the spinner GIF image, use `this.trigger` to make Backbone call the `showSpinner`:

```
this.trigger('spinner')
```

Next, we'll need to access the context inside of a closure. Sometimes I like to use a meaningful name instead of `_this` or `self`, so:

```
const view = this
```

Next, you would have an XHR call (e.g., `$.ajax()`) to the server to get the data. We'll simulate the real time lag when fetching data from the remote server with:

```
setTimeout(function ()  {
    view.model.set(view.collection.where({
      name:appleName
    })[0].attributes)
  }, 1000)
},
// ...
```

The `attributes` is a Backbone.js model property that gives a normal JavaScript object with the model's properties. To summarize, the line with `this.trigger('spinner')` will trigger the `spinner` event. We still have to write the function for this event.

The line `const view = this` after that is just for scoping issues. This give us the ability to use `appleView` inside of the subsequent callbacks/closures. And the `setTimeout` function is simulating a time lag of a real remote server response. Inside of it, we assign attributes of a selected model to our view's model by using a `model.set()` function and a `model.attributes` property (which returns the properties of a model).

Now we can remove extra code from the `render` method and implement the `showSpinner` function:

```
render: function(appleName) {
  const appleHtml = this.template(this.model)
  $('body').html(appleHtml)
},
showSpinner: function() {
  $('body').html(this.templateSpinner)
}
...
```

That's all! Open `index.html#apples/gala` or `index.html#apples/fuji` in your browser and enjoy the loading animation while waiting for an apple image to load.

Here is the full code of the `index.html` file (also in `04-backbone/binding/index.html` and at `http://bit.ly/2LhBNpx`):

```
<!DOCTYPE>
<html>
<head>
  <script src="jquery.js"></script>
  <script src="underscore.js"></script>
  <script src="backbone.js"></script>
```

```
<script>
  const appleData = [
    {
      name: 'fuji',
      url: 'img/fuji.jpg'
    },
    {
      name: 'gala',
      url: 'img/gala.jpg'
    }
  ]
  let app
  const router = Backbone.Router.extend({
    routes: {
      '': 'home',
      'apples/:appleName': 'loadApple'
    },
    initialize: function(){
      const apples = new Apples()
      apples.reset(appleData)
      this.homeView = new homeView({collection: apples})
      this.appleView = new appleView({collection:
      apples})
    },
    home: function(){
      this.homeView.render()
    },
    loadApple: function(appleName){
      this.appleView.loadApple(appleName)
    }
  })
```

```javascript
const homeView = Backbone.View.extend({
  el: 'body',
  template: _.template('Apple data: <%= data %>'),
  render: function(){
    this.$el.html(this.template({data: JSON.
    stringify(this.collection.models)}))
  }
})

const Apples = Backbone.Collection.extend({
})
const appleView = Backbone.View.extend({
  initialize: function(){
    this.model = new (Backbone.Model.extend({}))
    this.model.on('change', this.render, this)
    this.on('spinner', this.showSpinner, this)
  },
  template: _.template('<figure>\
                          <img src="<%= attributes.
                          url%>"/>\
                          <figcaption><%= attributes.
                          name %></figcaption>\
                        </figure>'),
  templateSpinner: '<img src="img/spinner.gif"
  width="30"/>',
  loadApple:function(appleName){
    this.trigger('spinner')
    const view = this
    setTimeout(function() {
      view.model.set(view.collection.where({name:
      appleName})[0].attributes)
    }, 1000)
  },
```

```
    render: function(appleName){
      const appleHtml = this.template(this.model)
      $('body').html(appleHtml)
    },
    showSpinner: function(){
      $('body').html(this.templateSpinner)
    }
  })

  $(document).ready(function(){
    app = new router
    Backbone.history.start()
  })

</script>
</head>
<body>
  <div></div>
</body>
</html>
```

Backbone.js Views and Subviews with Underscore.js

The example for this section is available in `code/04-backbone/subview` and at `http://bit.ly/2LhEOWH`.

Subviews are Backbone Views that are created and used inside of another Backbone View. A Subviews concept is a great way to abstract (separate) UI events (e.g., clicks), and templates for similarly structured elements (e.g., apples).

A use case of a Subview might include a row in a table, an item in a list, a paragraph, or a new line.

We'll refactor our home page to show a nice list of apples. Each list item will have an apple name and a Buy link with an `onClick` event. Let's start by creating a subview for a single apple with our standard Backbone `extend()` function:

```
// ...
const appleItemView = Backbone.View.extend({
  tagName: 'li',
  template: _.template(''
        +'<a href="#apples/<%=name%>"
        target="_blank">'
      +'<%=name%>'
      +'</a> <a class="add-to-cart"
      href="#">buy</a>'),
  events: {
    'click .add-to-cart': 'addToCart'
  },
  render: function() {
    this.$el.html(this.template(this.model.attributes))
  },
  addToCart: function() {
    this.model.collection.trigger('addToCart', this.
    model)
  }
})
// ...
```

Now we can populate the object with `tagName`, `template`, `events`, `render`, and `addToCart` properties and methods.

```
// ...
tagName: 'li',
// ...
```

tagName automatically allows Backbone.js to create an HTML element with the specified tag name, in this case `<li>` for list item. This will be a representation of a single apple, a row in our list.

```
// ...
template: _.template(''
       +'<a href="#apples/<%=name%>" target="_blank">'
     +'<%=name%>'
     +'</a> <a class="add-to-cart" href="#">buy</a>'),
// ...
```

The template is just a string with Underscore.js instructions. They are wrapped in `<%` and `%>` symbols. `<%=` simply means print a value. The same code can be written with backslash escapes:

```
// ...
template: _.template('\
     <a href="#apples/<%=name%>" target="_blank">\
     <%=name%>\
     </a> <a class="add-to-cart" href="#">buy</a>\
     '),
// ...
```

Each `<li>` will have two anchor elements (`<a>`), links to a detailed apple view (`#apples/:appleName`), and a Buy button. Now we're going to attach an event listener to the Buy button:

```
// ...
events: {
  'click .add-to-cart': 'addToCart'
},
// ...
```

The syntax follows this rule:

```
event + jQuery element selector: function name
```

Both the key and the value (right and left parts separated by the colon) are strings. For example:

```
'click .add-to-cart': 'addToCart'
```

or

```
'click #load-more': 'loadMoreData'
```

To render each item in the list, we'll use the jQuery `html()` function on the `this.$el` jQuery object, which is the `<li>` HTML element based on our `tagName` attribute:

```
// ...
render: function() {
  this.$el.html(this.template(this.model.attributes))
},
// ...
```

`addToCart` will use the `trigger()` function to notify the collection that this particular model (apple) is up for purchase by the user:

```
// ...
addToCart: function(){
  this.model.collection.trigger('addToCart', this.model)
}
// ...
```

Here is the full code of the `appleItemView` Backbone View class:

```
// ...
const appleItemView = Backbone.View.extend({
  tagName: 'li',
```

```
template: _.template(''
        + '<a href="#apples/<%=name%>" target="_blank">'
    + '<%=name%>'
    + '</a> <a class="add-to-cart" href="#">buy
    </a>'),
events: {
  'click .add-to-cart': 'addToCart'
},
render: function() {
  this.$el.html(this.template(this.model.attributes))
},
addToCart: function(){
  this.model.collection.trigger('addToCart', this.model)
}
})
// ...
```

Easy peasy! But what about the master view, which is supposed to render all of our items (apples) and provide a wrapper <ul> container for li HTML elements? We need to modify and enhance our homeView.

To begin with, we can add extra properties of string type understandable by jQuery as selectors to homeView:

```
// ...
el: 'body',
listEl: '.apples-list',
cartEl: '.cart-box',
// ...
```

We can use properties from earlier in the template, or just hard-code them (we'll refactor our code later) in `homeView`:

```
// ...
template: _.template('Apple data: \
  <ul class="apples-list">\
  </ul>\
  <div class="cart-box"></div>'),
// ...
```

The `initialize` function will be called when `homeView` is created (`new homeView()`). There we render our template (with our favorite `html()` function), and attach an event listener to the collection, which is a set of apple models:

```
// ...
initialize: function() {
  this.$el.html(this.template)
  this.collection.on('addToCart', this.showCart, this)
},
// ...
```

The syntax for the binding event is covered in the previous section. In essence, it is calling the `showCart()` function of `homeView`. In this function, we append `appleName` to the cart (along with a line break, a `<br/>` element):

```
// ...
showCart: function(appleModel) {
  $(this.cartEl).append(appleModel.attributes.name + '<br/>')
},
// ...
```

Finally, here is our long-awaited `render()` method, in which we iterate through each model in the collection (each apple), create an `appleItemView` for each apple, create an `<li>` element for each apple, and append that element to `view.listEl` — `<ul>` element with a class `apples-list` in the DOM:

```
// ...
render: function() {
  view = this
  // So we can use view inside of closure
  this.collection.each(function(apple){
    const appleSubView = new appleItemView({model:apple})
    // Creates subview with model apple
    appleSubView.render()
    // Compiles template and single apple data
    $(view.listEl).append(appleSubView.$el)
    // Append jQuery object from single
    // Apple to apples-list DOM element
  })
}
// ...
```

Let's make sure we didn't miss anything in the `homeView` Backbone View. Here's the full code sans the inline comments:

```
// ...
const homeView = Backbone.View.extend({
  el: 'body',
  listEl: '.apples-list',
  cartEl: '.cart-box',
  template: _.template('Apple data: \
    <ul class="apples-list">\
    </ul>\
    <div class="cart-box"></div>'),
```

```
initialize: function() {
  this.$el.html(this.template)
  this.collection.on('addToCart', this.showCart, this)
},
showCart: function(appleModel) {
  $(this.cartEl).append(appleModel.attributes.name +
  '<br/>')
},
render: function() {
  view = this
  this.collection.each(function(apple) {
    const appleSubView = new appleItemView({model:
    apple})
    appleSubView.render()
    $(view.listEl).append(appleSubView.$el)
  })
}
})
// ...
```

You should be able to click the Buy button and populate the cart with the apples of your choice. Looking at an individual apple does not require typing its name in the URL address bar of the browser anymore. We can click the name to open a new window with a detailed view.

By using subviews, we reused the template for all of the items (apples) and attached a specific event to each of them (see Figure 4-1). Those events are smart enough to pass the information about the model to other objects: views and collections.

Apple data:

- <u>fuji</u> <u>buy</u>
- <u>gala</u> <u>buy</u>

gala
fuji
fuji
fuji
fuji
fuji
gala
gala
gala
gala
gala

Figure 4-1. *The list of apples rendered by subviews*

Just in case, here is the full code for the subviews example, which is also available at `http://bit.ly/2LhEOWH`:

```html
<!DOCTYPE>
<html>
<head>
  <script src="jquery.js"></script>
  <script src="underscore.js"></script>
  <script src="backbone.js"></script>

  <script>
    const appleData = [
      {
        name: 'fuji',
        url: 'img/fuji.jpg'
      },
```

```
      {
        name: 'gala',
        url: 'img/gala.jpg'
      }
    ]
    let app
    const router = Backbone.Router.extend({
      routes: {
        '': 'home',
        'apples/:appleName': 'loadApple'
      },
      initialize: function(){
        const apples = new Apples()
        apples.reset(appleData)
        this.homeView = new homeView({collection: apples})
        this.appleView = new appleView({collection: apples})
      },
      home: function(){
        this.homeView.render()
      },
      loadApple: function(appleName){
        this.appleView.loadApple(appleName)

      }
    })
    const appleItemView = Backbone.View.extend({
      tagName: 'li',
      template: _.template('\
            <a href="#apples/<%=name%>" target="_blank">\
          <%=name%>\
          </a> <a class="add-to-cart" href="#">\
          buy</a>\
          '),
```

```
  events: {
    'click .add-to-cart': 'addToCart'
  },
  render: function() {
    this.$el.html(this.template(this.model.attributes))
  },
  addToCart: function(){
    this.model.collection.trigger('addToCart', this.
    model)
  }
})

const homeView = Backbone.View.extend({
  el: 'body',
  listEl: '.apples-list',
  cartEl: '.cart-box',
  template: _.template('Apple data: \
    <ul class="apples-list">\
    </ul>\
    <div class="cart-box"></div>'),
  initialize: function() {
    this.$el.html(this.template)
    this.collection.on('addToCart', this.showCart,
    this)
  },
  showCart: function(appleModel) {
    $(this.cartEl).append(appleModel.attributes.name +
    '<br/>')
  },
  render: function(){
    view = this
```

```
    this.collection.each(function(apple){
      const appleSubView = new appleItemView({model:
      apple})
      appleSubView.render()
      $(view.listEl).append(appleSubView.$el)
    })
  }
})
const Apples = Backbone.Collection.extend({
})
const appleView = Backbone.View.extend({
  initialize: function(){
    this.model = new (Backbone.Model.extend({}))
    this.model.on('change', this.render, this)
    this.on('spinner', this.showSpinner, this)
  },
  template: _.template('<figure>\
                        <img src="<%= attributes.
                        url%>"/>\
                        <figcaption><%= attributes.
                        name %></figcaption>\
                      </figure>'),
  templateSpinner: '<img src="img/spinner.gif"
  width="30"/>',
  loadApple:function(appleName){
    this.trigger('spinner')
    const view = this
    setTimeout(function(){
      view.model.set(view.collection.where({name:
      appleName})[0].attributes)
    }, 1000)
  },
```

```
render: function(appleName){
  const appleHtml = this.template(this.model)
  $('body').html(appleHtml)
},
showSpinner: function(){
  $('body').html(this.templateSpinner)
}
})

$(document).ready(function(){
  app = new router
  Backbone.history.start()
})
</script>
</head>
<body>
  <div></div>
</body>
</html>
```

The link to an individual item, for example, `collections/index.html#apples/fuji`, also should work independently, by typing it in the browser address bar.

Refactoring Backbone.js Code

At this point you are probably wondering what the benefit is of using the framework and still having multiple classes, objects, and elements with different functionalities in one single file. This was done for the purpose of adhering to the idea of keeping things simple.

The bigger your application is, the more pain there is in an unorganized code base. Let's break down our application into multiple files where each file will be one of these types:

- View

- Template

- Router

- Collection

- Model

Let's write these scripts to include tags into our `index.html` head, or body, as noted previously:

```
<script src="apple-item.view.js"></script>
<script src="apple-home.view.js"></script>
<script src="apple.view.js"></script>
<script src="apples.js"></script>
<script src="apple-app.js"></script>
```

The names don't have to follow the convention of dashes and dots, as long as it's easy to tell what each file is supposed to do.

Now, let's copy our objects and classes into the corresponding files.

Our main `index.html` file should look very minimalistic:

```
<!DOCTYPE>
<html>
<head>
  <script src="jquery.js"></script>
  <script src="underscore.js"></script>
  <script src="backbone.js"></script>

  <script src="apple-item.view.js"></script>
  <script src="apple-home.view.js"></script>
```

```html
    <script src="apple.view.js"></script>
    <script src="apples.js"></script>
    <script src="apple-app.js"></script>

</head>
<body>
  <div></div>
</body>
</html>
```

The other files just have the code that corresponds to their file names.
The content of `apple-item.view.js` will have the `appleView` object:

```js
const appleView = Backbone.View.extend({
  initialize: function(){
    this.model = new (Backbone.Model.extend({}))
    this.model.on('change', this.render, this)
    this.on('spinner', this.showSpinner, this)
  },
  template: _.template('<figure>\
          <img src="<%= attributes.url %>"/>\
          <figcaption><%= attributes.name %>
          </figcaption>\
        </figure>'),
  templateSpinner: '<img src="img/spinner.gif"
  width="30"/>',

  loadApple:function(appleName){
    this.trigger('spinner')
    const view = this
    // We'll need to access that inside of a closure
```

```
    setTimeout(function(){
    // Simulates real time lag when fetching
    // data from the remote server
      view.model.set(view.collection.where({
        name: appleName
      })[0].attributes)
    }, 1000)
  },

  render: function(appleName){
    const appleHtml = this.template(this.model)
    $('body').html(appleHtml)
  },
  showSpinner: function(){
    $('body').html(this.templateSpinner)
  }
})
```

The `apple-home.view.js` file has the `homeView` object:

```
const homeView = Backbone.View.extend({
  el: 'body',
  listEl: '.apples-list',
  cartEl: '.cart-box',
  template: _.template('Apple data: \
    <ul class="apples-list">\
    </ul>\
    <div class="cart-box"></div>'),
  initialize: function() {
    this.$el.html(this.template)
    this.collection.on('addToCart', this.showCart, this)
  },
```

```javascript
showCart: function(appleModel) {
  $(this.cartEl).append(appleModel.attributes.name +
  '<br/>')
},
render: function(){
  view = this // So we can use view inside of closure
  this.collection.each(function(apple){
    const appleSubView = new
    appleItemView({model:apple})
    // Create subview with model apple
    appleSubView.render()
    // Compiles template and single apple data
    $(view.listEl).append(appleSubView.$el)
    // Append jQuery object from
    // single apple to apples-list DOM element
  })
}
})
```

The `apple.view.js` file contains the master apples list:

```javascript
const appleView = Backbone.View.extend({
  initialize: function() {
    this.model = new (Backbone.Model.extend({}))
    this.model.on('change', this.render, this)
    this.on('spinner',this.showSpinner, this)
  },
  template: _.template('<figure>\
        <img src="<%= attributes.url %>"/>\
        <figcaption><%= attributes.name %></figcaption>\
      </figure>'),
  templateSpinner: '<img src="img/spinner.gif"
  width="30"/>',
```

```javascript
loadApple:function(appleName) {
  this.trigger('spinner')
  const view = this
  // We'll need to access that inside of a closure
  setTimeout(function() {
  // Simulates real time lag when
  // fetching data from the remote server
    view.model.set(view.collection.where({
      name:appleName
    })[0].attributes)
  }, 1000)
},
render: function(appleName) {
  const appleHtml = this.template(this.model)
  $('body').html(appleHtml)
},
showSpinner: function() {
  $('body').html(this.templateSpinner)
}
})
```

`apples.js` is an empty collection:

```javascript
const Apples = Backbone.Collection.extend({
})
```

`apple-app.js` is the main application file with the data, the router, and the starting command:

```javascript
const appleData = [
  {
    name: 'fuji',
    url: 'img/fuji.jpg'
  },
```

164

```
  {
    name: 'gala',
    url: 'img/gala.jpg'
  }
]
let app
const router = Backbone.Router.extend({
  routes: {
    '': 'home',
    'apples/:appleName': 'loadApple'
  },
  initialize: function() {
    const apples = new Apples()
    apples.reset(appleData)
    this.homeView = new homeView({collection: apples})
    this.appleView = new appleView({collection: apples})
  },
  home: function() {
    this.homeView.render()
  },
  loadApple: function(appleName) {
    this.appleView.loadApple(appleName)
  }
})
$(document).ready(function() {
  app = new router
  Backbone.history.start()
})
```

Now let's try to open the application. It should work exactly the same as in the previous Subviews example.

It's a far better code organization, but it's still far from perfect, because we still have HTML templates directly in the JavaScript code. The problem is that designers and developers can't work on the same files, and any change to the presentation requires a change in the main code base.

We can add a few more JS files to our `index.html` file:

```
<script src="apple-item.tpl.js"></script>
<script src="apple-home.tpl.js"></script>
<script src="apple-spinner.tpl.js"></script>
<script src="apple.tpl.js"></script>
```

Usually, one Backbone View has one template, but in the case of our `appleView`—a detailed view of an apple in a separate window—we also have a spinner, a "loading" GIF animation.

The contents of the files are just global variables that are assigned some string values. Later we can use these variables in our views, when we call the Underscore.js helper method `.template()`.

Here is the `apple-item.tpl.js` file:

```
const appleItemTpl = '\
    <a href="#apples/<%=name%>" target="_blank">\
  <%=name%>\
  </a> <a class="add-to-cart" href="#">buy</a>\
    '
```

This is the `apple-home.tpl.js` file:

```
const appleHomeTpl = 'Apple data: \
    <ul class="apples-list">\
    </ul>\
    <div class="cart-box"></div>'
```

Here is the `apple-spinner.tpl.js` file:

```
const appleSpinnerTpl = '<img src="img/spinner.gif"
width="30"/>'
```

This is the `apple.tpl.js` file:

```
const appleTpl = '<figure>\
            <img src="<%= attributes.url %>"/>\
            <figcaption><%= attributes.name %>
            </figcaption>\
        </figure>'
```

Try to start the application now. The full code is at `http://bit.ly/2LdEtEy`.

As you can see in the previous example, we used global scoped variables (without the keyword `window`).

Be careful when you introduce a lot of variables into the global namespace (`window` keyword). There might be conflicts and other unpredictable consequences. For example, if you wrote an open source library and other developers started using the methods and properties directly, instead of using the interface, what would happen later when you decide to finally remove or deprecate those global leaks? To prevent this, properly written libraries and applications use JavaScript closures (`https://developer.mozilla.org/en-US/docs/Web/JavaScript/Closures`).

Here is an example of using closure and a global variable module definition:

```
;(function() {
  const apple = function() {
  ...// Do something useful like return apple object
  }
  window.Apple = apple
}())
```

In a case when we need to access the `app` object (which creates a dependency on that object):

```
; (function() {
  let app = this.app
<<[] [/ Equivalent of window.application]
  // in case we need a dependency (app)
  this.apple = function() {

    ...
    // Return apple object/class
    // Use app variable
  }
  // Equivalent of window.apple = function(){...}
} ())
```

As you can see, we've created the function and called it immediately while also wrapping everything in parentheses `()`.

AMD and Require.js for Backbone.js Development

AMD allows us to organize development code into modules, manage dependencies, and load them asynchronously. The article "Why AMD" does a great job at explaining benefits of AMD: `http://requirejs.org/docs/whyamd.html`.

Start your local HTTP server, for example, MAMP (`https://www.mamp.info`) or `node-static` (`https://npmjs.com/node-static`).

Let's enhance our code by using the Require.js library.

Our `index.html` will shrink even more:

```html
<!DOCTYPE>
<html>
  <head>
    <script src="jquery.js"></script>
    <script src="underscore.js"></script>
    <script src="backbone.js"></script>
    <script src="require.js"></script>
    <script src="apple-app.js"></script>
  </head>
  <body>
    <div></div>
  </body>
</html>
```

We only included libraries and the single JavaScript file with our application. This file has the following structure:

```
require([...],function(...){...})
```

In a more explanatory way:

```
require([
  'name-of-the-module',
  ...
  'name-of-the-other-module'
],function(referenceToModule, ...,
referenceToOtherModule){
// Some useful code...
referenceToModule.someMethod()
})
```

Basically, we tell a browser to load the files from the array of file names—the first parameter of the `require()` function—and then pass our modules from those files to the anonymous callback function (second argument) as variables. Inside of the main function (anonymous callback) we can use our modules by referencing those variables. Therefore, our `apple-app.js` metamorphoses into:

```
require([
  'apple-item.tpl', // Can use shim plug-in
  'apple-home.tpl',
  'apple-spinner.tpl',
  'apple.tpl',
  'apple-item.view',
  'apple-home.view',
  'apple.view',
  'apples'
], function(
  appleItemTpl,
  appleHomeTpl,
  appleSpinnerTpl,
  appleTpl,
  appleItemView,
  homeView,
  appleView,
  Apples
){
  const appleData = [
    {
      name: 'fuji',
      url: 'img/fuji.jpg'
    },
```

```
    {
      name: 'gala',
      url: 'img/gala.jpg'
    }
  ]
  let app
  const router = Backbone.Router.extend({
  // Check if need to be required
    routes: {
      '': 'home',
      'apples/:appleName': 'loadApple'
    },
    initialize: function() {
      const apples = new Apples()
      apples.reset(appleData)
      this.homeView = new homeView({collection: apples})
      this.appleView = new appleView({collection: apples})
    },
    home: function() {
      this.homeView.render()
    },
    loadApple: function(appleName) {
      this.appleView.loadApple(appleName)
    }
  })

  $(document).ready(function() {
    app = new router
    Backbone.history.start()
  })
})
```

We put all of the code inside the function that is a second argument of `require()`, mentioned modules by their file names, and used dependencies via corresponding parameters. Now we should define the module itself. This is how we can do it with the `define()` method:

```
define([...],function(...) {...})
```

The meaning is similar to the `require()` function: Dependencies are strings of file names (and paths) in the array that is passed as the first argument. The second argument is the main function that accepts other libraries as parameters (the order of parameters and modules in the array is important):

```
define(['name-of-the-module'],function(nameOfModule) {
  const b = nameOfModule.render()
  return b
})
```

Note that there is no need to append `.js` to file names. Require.js does it automatically. The Shim plug-in is used for importing text files such as HTML templates.

Let's start with the templates and convert them into the Require.js modules.

Here is the new `apple-item.tpl.js` file:

```
define(function() {
  return '\
          <a href="#apples/<%=name%>"
          target="_blank">\
        <%=name%>\
        </a> <a class="add-to-cart"
        href="#">buy</a>\
        '
})
```

This is the `apple-home.tpl` file:

```
define(function() {
  return 'Apple data: \
        <ul class="apples-list">\
        </ul>\
        <div class="cart-box"></div>'
})
```

Here is the `apple-spinner.tpl.js` file:

```
define(function() {
  return '<img src="img/spinner.gif" width="30"/>'
})
```

This is the `apple.tpl.js` file:

```
define(function() {
  return '<figure>\
        <img src="<%= attributes.url %>"/>\
        <figcaption><%= attributes.name %></figcaption>\
      </figure>'
  })
```

Here is the `apple-item.view.js` file:

```
define(function() {
  return '\
            <a href="#apples/<%=name%>"
            target="_blank">\
          <%=name%>\
          </a> <a class="add-to-cart"
          href="#">buy</a>\
          '
})
```

In the `apple-home.view.js` file, we need to declare dependencies on `apple-home.tpl` and `apple-item.view.js` files:

```
define(['apple-home.tpl', 'apple-item.view'], function(
  appleHomeTpl,
  appleItemView){
return Backbone.View.extend({
     el: 'body',
     listEl: '.apples-list',
     cartEl: '.cart-box',
     template: _.template(appleHomeTpl),
     initialize: function() {
       this.$el.html(this.template)
       this.collection.on('addToCart', this.showCart,
       this)
     },
     showCart: function(appleModel) {
       $(this.cartEl).append(appleModel.attributes.name +
       '<br/>')
     },
     render: function() {
       view = this // So we can use view inside of
       closure
       this.collection.each(function(apple){
         const appleSubView = new
         appleItemView({model:apple})
         // Create subview with model apple
         appleSubView.render()
         // Compiles template and single apple data
         $(view.listEl).append(appleSubView.$el)
```

```
          // Append jQuery object from
          // a single apple to apples-list DOM element
        })
      }
    })
})
```

The `apple.view.js` file depends on two templates:

```
define([
  'apple.tpl',
  'apple-spinner.tpl'
], function(appleTpl, appleSpinnerTpl) {
  return Backbone.View.extend({
    initialize: function() {
      this.model = new (Backbone.Model.extend({}))
      this.model.on('change', this.render, this)
      this.on('spinner', this.showSpinner, this)
    },
    template: _.template(appleTpl),
    templateSpinner: appleSpinnerTpl,
    loadApple:function(appleName) {
      this.trigger('spinner')
      const view = this
      // We'll need to access that inside of a closure
      setTimeout(function() {
      // Simulates real time lag when
      // fetching data from the remote server
        view.model.set(view.collection.where({
          name:appleName
        })[0].attributes)
      }, 1000)
    },
```

```
  render: function(appleName){
    const appleHtml = this.template(this.model)
    $('body').html(appleHtml)
  },
  showSpinner: function(){
    $('body').html(this.templateSpinner)
  }
})
})
```

This is the `apples.js` file:

```
define(function() {
  return Backbone.Collection.extend({})
})
```

I hope you can see the pattern by now. All of our code is split into the separate files based on the logic (e.g., view class, collection class, template). The main file loads all of the dependencies with the `require()` function. If we need some module in a non-main file, then we can ask for it in the `define()` method. Usually, in modules we want to return an object; for example, in templates we return strings and in views we return Backbone View classes and objects.

Try launching the example located in `code/04-backbone/amd` and at `http://bit.ly/2LhEmb9`. Visually, there shouldn't be any changes. If you open the Network tab in the Developers Tool, you can see a difference in how the files are loaded.

The old file shown in Figure 4-2 (`code/04-backbone/refactor/index.html` and `http://bit.ly/2Lfi7lT`) loads our JavaScript scripts in a serial manner, whereas the new file shown in Figure 4-3 (`code/04-backbone/amd/index.html`) loads them in parallel.

Apple data:

- fuji buy
- gala buy

Name Path	Method	Status Text	Type	Initiator	Size Content	Time Latency	Timeline	166 ms	250 ms	333 ms	416 ms	499 ms
index.html /General%20Assembly/ga-backbone/	GET	200 OK	text/html	Other	(from cac...	4 ms 4 ms						
jquery.js /General%20Assembly/ga-backbone/	GET	200 OK	applicatio...	index.html:4 Parser	261 KB 261 KB	54 ms 10 ms						
underscore.js /General%20Assembly/ga-backbone/	GET	200 OK	applicatio...	index.html:4 Parser	40.7 KB 40.4 KB	38 ms 10 ms						
backbone.js /General%20Assembly/ga-backbone/	GET	200 OK	applicatio...	index.html:4 Parser	54.8 KB 54.5 KB	41 ms 29 ms						
apple-item.tpl.js /General%20Assembly/ga-backbone/	GET	200 OK	applicatio...	index.html:4 Parser	469 B 181 B	37 ms 28 ms						
apple-spinner.tpl.js /General%20Assembly/ga-backbone/	GET	200 OK	applicatio...	index.html:4 Parser	351 B 64 B	60 ms 41 ms						
apple-home.view.js /General%20Assembly/ga-backbone/	GET	200 OK	applicatio...	index.html:4 Parser	1.1 KB 878 B	61 ms 43 ms						
apple.tpl.js /General%20Assembly/ga-backbone/	GET	200 OK	applicatio...	index.html:4 Parser	496 B 209 B	60 ms 41 ms						
apple-item.view.js /General%20Assembly/ga-backbone/	GET	200 OK	applicatio...	index.html:4 Parser	867 B 579 B	58 ms 38 ms						
apple-home.tpl.js /General%20Assembly/ga-backbone/	GET	200 OK	applicatio...	index.html:4 Parser	409 B 121 B	116 ms 69 ms						
apples.js /General%20Assembly/ga-backbone/	GET	200 OK	applicatio...	index.html:4 Parser	342 B 56 B	113 ms 61 ms						
apple.view.js /General%20Assembly/ga-backbone/	GET	200 OK	applicatio...	index.html:4 Parser	1.2 KB 910 B	111 ms 49 ms						
apple-app.js /General%20Assembly/ga-backbone/	GET	200 OK	applicatio...	index.html:4 Parser	1.1 KB 813 B	112 ms 60 ms						
nudge-icon-arrow-up.png pioclpoplcdbaefihamjohnefbikjilc/ima	GET	200 OK	image/png	Preview.js:41 Script	(from cac...	0 ms 0 ms						
nudge-icon-arrow-down.png	GET	200	image/png	Preview.js:41 Script	(from cac...	0 ms						

Figure 4-2. *The old 04-backbone/refactor/index.html file*

Apple data:

- fuji buy
- gala buy

Figure 4-3. *The new 04-backbone/amd/index.html file*

Require.js has a lot of configuration options that are defined through the `requirejs.config()` call in the top level of an HTML page. More information can be found at `http://requirejs.org/docs/api.html#config`.

Let's add a bust parameter to our example. The bust argument will be appended to the URL of each file, preventing a browser from caching the files. This is perfect for development and terrible for production.

Add this to the `apple-app.js` file in front of everything else:

```
requirejs.config({
  urlArgs: 'bust=' + (new Date()).getTime()
})
require([
// ...
```

Notice in Figure 4-4 that each file request now has status 200 instead of 304 (not modified).

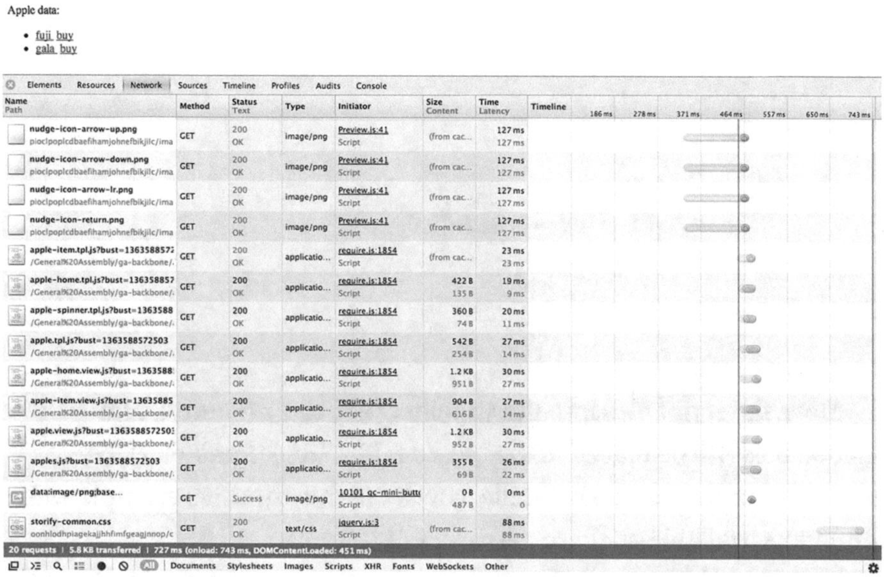

Figure 4-4. *Network tab with bust parameter added*

Require.js for Backbone.js Production

We'll use the Node.js package manager (npm) to install the `requirejs` library (it's not a typo; there's no period in the name). In your project folder, run this command in a terminal:

```
$ npm init
```

Then run

```
$ npm install requirejs
```

or add `-g` for global installation:

```
$ npm install -g requirejs
```

Create a file named `app.build.js`:

```
({
    appDir: "./js",
    baseUrl: "./",
    dir: "build",
    modules: [
        {
            name: "apple-app"
        }
    ]
})
```

Move the script files into the `js` folder (`appDir` property). The builded files will be placed in the `build` folder (`dir` parameter). For more information on the build file, check out the extensive example with comments available at `http://bit.ly/2LdFSuO`.

Now everything should be ready for building one gigantic JavaScript file that will include all of our dependencies and modules:

```
$ r.js -o app.build.js
```

or

```
$ node_modules/requirejs/bin/r.js -o app.build.js
```

You should get a list of the `r.js` processed files, as shown in Figure 4-5.

```
Uglifying file: /Users/azat/Documents/Development/General Assembly/ga-backbone/r/build/apple-app.js
Uglifying file: /Users/azat/Documents/Development/General Assembly/ga-backbone/r/build/apple-home.tpl.js
Uglifying file: /Users/azat/Documents/Development/General Assembly/ga-backbone/r/build/apple-home.view.js
Uglifying file: /Users/azat/Documents/Development/General Assembly/ga-backbone/r/build/apple-item.tpl.js
Uglifying file: /Users/azat/Documents/Development/General Assembly/ga-backbone/r/build/apple-item.view.js
Uglifying file: /Users/azat/Documents/Development/General Assembly/ga-backbone/r/build/apple-spinner.tpl.js
Uglifying file: /Users/azat/Documents/Development/General Assembly/ga-backbone/r/build/apple.tpl.js
Uglifying file: /Users/azat/Documents/Development/General Assembly/ga-backbone/r/build/apple.view.js
Uglifying file: /Users/azat/Documents/Development/General Assembly/ga-backbone/r/build/apples.js
Uglifying file: /Users/azat/Documents/Development/General Assembly/ga-backbone/r/build/backbone.js
Uglifying file: /Users/azat/Documents/Development/General Assembly/ga-backbone/r/build/jquery.js
toTransport skipping /Users/azat/Documents/Development/General Assembly/ga-backbone/r/build/node_modules/.bin/r.js: Error: Line 1: Unexpe
cted token ILLEGAL
Error: Cannot parse file: /Users/azat/Documents/Development/General Assembly/ga-backbone/r/build/node_modules/.bin/r.js for comments. Ski
pping it. Error is:
Error: Line 1: Unexpected token ILLEGAL
toTransport skipping /Users/azat/Documents/Development/General Assembly/ga-backbone/r/build/node_modules/requirejs/bin/r.js: Error: Line
1: Unexpected token ILLEGAL
Error: Cannot parse file: /Users/azat/Documents/Development/General Assembly/ga-backbone/r/build/node_modules/requirejs/bin/r.js for comm
ents. Skipping it. Error is:
Error: Line 1: Unexpected token ILLEGAL
Uglifying file: /Users/azat/Documents/Development/General Assembly/ga-backbone/r/build/node_modules/requirejs/require.js
Uglifying file: /Users/azat/Documents/Development/General Assembly/ga-backbone/r/build/require.js
Uglifying file: /Users/azat/Documents/Development/General Assembly/ga-backbone/r/build/underscore.js

apple-app.js
----------------
apple-item.tpl.js
apple-home.tpl.js
apple-spinner.tpl.js
apple.tpl.js
apple-item.view.js
apple-home.view.js
apple.view.js
apples.js
apple-app.js

◆ r git:(master) ✗ $ node_modules/requirejs/bin/r.js -o app.build.js
```

Figure 4-5. *A list of the r.js processed files*

Open `index.html` from the build folder in a browser window, and check if the Network tab shows any improvement now with just one request or file to load (Figure 4-6).

Apple data:

- fuji buy
- gala buy

Name Path	Method	Status Text	Type	Initiator	Size Content	Time Latency	Timeline	139 ms	208 ms	277 ms	347 ms	416 ms	485 ms	555 ms
index.html /General%20Assembly/ga-backbone/	GET	304 Not Modified	text/html	Other	(from cac...	4 ms 4 ms								
jquery.js /General%20Assembly/ga-backbone/	GET	304 Not Modified	applicatio...	index.html:4 Parser	173 B 91.3 KB	10 ms 5 ms								
underscore.js /General%20Assembly/ga-backbone/	GET	304 Not Modified	applicatio...	index.html:4 Parser	173 B 13.4 KB	8 ms 6 ms								
backbone.js /General%20Assembly/ga-backbone/	GET	304 Not Modified	applicatio...	index.html:4 Parser	173 B 18.0 KB	8 ms 6 ms								
require.js /General%20Assembly/ga-backbone/	GET	304 Not Modified	applicatio...	index.html:4 Parser	173 B 16.1 KB	9 ms 6 ms								
apple-app.js /General%20Assembly/ga-backbone/	GET	304 Not Modified	applicatio...	index.html:4 Parser	172 B 2.7 KB	80 ms 18 ms								
nudge-i http://localhost/General%20Assembly/ga- pioclpopbackbone/r/build/apple-app.js	GET	200 OK	image/png	Preview.js:41 Script	(from cac...	134 ms 134 ms								
nudge-icon-arrow-down.png pioclpopicdbaeflhamjohnefbikjilc/ima	GET	200 OK	image/png	Preview.js:41 Script	(from cac...	134 ms 134 ms								
nudge-icon-arrow-lr.png pioclpopicdbaeflhamjohnefbikjilc/ima	GET	200 OK	image/png	Preview.js:41 Script	(from cac...	134 ms 134 ms								
nudge-icon-return.png pioclpopicdbaeflhamjohnefbikjilc/ima	GET	200 OK	image/png	Preview.js:41 Script	(from cac...	132 ms 132 ms								
data:image/png;base...	GET	Success	image/png	10101 gc-mini-butt Script	(from cac...	0 ms 0 ms								
storify-common.css oonhlodhpiagekajihhfimfgeaginnop/c	GET	200 OK	text/css	jquery.js:3 Script	(from cac...	0 ms 0 ms								

12 requests | 864 B transferred | 555 ms (onload: 426 ms, DOMContentLoaded: 406 ms)

All | Documents   Stylesheets   Images   Scripts   XHR   Fonts   WebSockets   Other

Figure 4-6. *Performance improvement with one request or file to load*

For more information, check out the official `r.js` documentation at `http://requirejs.org/docs/optimization.html`.

The example code is available at `http://bit.ly/2LiMuYM` and `http://bit.ly/2Lg6efx`.

For uglification of JS files (which decreases the file sizes), we can use the Uglify2 module. To install it with npm, use:

```
$ npm install uglify-js
```

Then update the `app.build.js` file with the `optimize: "uglify2"` property:

```
({
    appDir: "./js",
    baseUrl: "./",
    dir: "build",
    optimize: "uglify2",
```

```
    modules: [
        {
            name: "apple-app"
        }
    ]
})
```

Run r.js with:

```
$ node_modules/requirejs/bin/r.js -o app.build.js
```

You should get something like this:

```
define("apple-item.tpl",[],function(){return'
<a href="#apples/<%=name%>" target="_blank"> <%=name%>
</a> <a class="add-to-cart" href="#">buy
</a>'}),define("apple-home.tpl",[],function(){return
'Apple data: <ul class="apples-list"> </ul>
<div class="cart-box"></div>'}),define("apple-spinner.tpl",
[],function(){return'<img src="img/spinner.gif"
width="30"/>'}),define("apple.tpl",[],function()
{return'<figure> <img src="<%= attributes.url %>"/>
<figcaption><%= attributes.name %></figcaption>
</figure>'}),define("apple-item.view",["apple-item.
tpl"],function(e){return Backbone.View.extend({tagName:
"li",template:_.template(e),events:{"click .add-to-car
t":"addToCart"},render:function(){this.$el.html(this.
template(this.model.attributes))},addToCart:function
(){this.model.collection.trigger("addToCart",this.
model)}})}),define("apple-home.view",["apple-
home.tpl","apple-item.view"],function(e,t){return
Backbone.View.extend({el:"body",listEl:".apples-
list",cartEl:".cart-box",template:_.template(e),
initialize:function(){this.$el.html(this.template),this.
```

```
collection.on("addToCart",this.showCart,this)},
showCart:function(e){$(this.cartEl).append(e.attributes.
name+"<br/>")},render:function(){view=this,this.
collection.each(function(e){const i=new t({model:e});
i.render(),$(view.listEl).append(i.$el)})}})}}),define
("apple.view",["apple.tpl","apple-spinner.tpl"],function(e,t)
{return Backbone.View.extend({initialize:function()
{this.model=new(Backbone.Model.extend({})),this.model.
on("change",this.render,this),this.on("spinner",this.
showSpinner,this)},template:_.template(e),templateSpinner:t,
loadApple:function(e){this.trigger("spinner");const
t=this;setTimeout(function(){t.model.set(t.collection.
where({name:e})[0].attributes)},1e3)},render:function()
{const e=this.template(this.model);$("body").html(e)},
showSpinner:function(){$("body").html(this.templateSpinner)
}})}),define("apples",[],function(){return Backbone.
Collection.extend({})}),requirejs.config({urlArgs:"bust="
+(new Date).getTime()}),require(["apple-item.tpl","apple-
home.tpl","apple-spinner.tpl","apple.tpl","apple-item.
view","apple-home.view","apple.view","apples"],function
(e,t,i,n,a,l,p,o){const r,s=[{name:"fuji",url:"img/
fuji.jpg"},{name:"gala",url:"img/gala.jpg"}],c=Backbone.
Router.extend({routes:{"":"home","apples/:appleName"
:"loadApple"},initialize:function(){const e=new o;e.
reset(s),this.homeView=new l({collection:e}),this.
appleView=new p({collection:e})},home:function()
{this.homeView.render()},loadApple:function(e){this.
appleView.loadApple(e)}});$(document).ready(function()
{r=new c,Backbone.history.start()})}),define("apple-
app",function(){});
```

The file is intentionally not formatted to show how Uglify2 works (`https://npmjs.com/uglify-js` and `http://lisperator.net/uglifyjs`). Without the line break escape symbols, the code is on one line. Also notice that variables' and objects' names are shortened.

Super Simple Backbone.js Starter Kit

To jump-start your Backbone.js development, consider using Super Simple Backbone Starter Kit (`http://bit.ly/2LhjDE4`) or similar projects:

- Backbone Boilerplate available at `http://backboneboilerplate.com`

- Sample App with Backbone.js and Bootstrap available at `http://coenraets.org/blog/2012/02/sample-app-with-backbone-js-and-twitter-bootstrap`

- More Backbone.js tutorials available at `http://bit.ly/2LfBifE`

Summary

So far we've covered how to:

- Build a Backbone.js application from scratch.

- Use views, collections, subviews, models, and event binding.

- Use AMD and Require.js on the example of the apple database application.

In this chapter, you've learned enough about Backbone.js to make sure you can start using it in your web or mobile apps. Without a framework like Backbone, your code will become exponentially more complex as it grows. On the other hand, with Backbone or a similar MVC architecture, you can scale the code better.

CHAPTER 5

Backbone.js and Parse

When in doubt—console log.

—Azat Mardan

In this chapter, we'll explore the practical aspect of leveraging Parse for a Backbone.js app. The chapter will illustrate the following:

- Backbone.js and Parse usage

- Modifying Message Board with Parse and JavaScript SDK

- Taking Message Board further the

If you've written some complex client-side applications, you might have found that it's challenging to maintain the spaghetti code of JavaScript callbacks and UI events. Backbone.js provides a lightweight yet powerful way to organize your logic into a Model-View-Controller (MVC) type of structure. It also has nice features like URL routing, REST API support, event listeners, and triggers. For more information and step-by-step examples of building Backbone.js applications from scratch, please refer to Chapter 4 "Intro to Backbone.js."

© Azat Mardan 2018
A. Mardan, *Full Stack JavaScript*, https://doi.org/10.1007/978-1-4842-3718-2_5

Message Board with Parse: JavaScript SDK and Backbone.js Version

Speaking of Message Board with jQuery that I covered earlier, it's easy to see that if we keep adding more and more buttons such as "DELETE," "UPDATE," and other functionalities, our asynchronous callbacks will grow more complicated. And we'll have to know when to update the view (i.e., the list of messages) based on whether or not there were changes to the data. The Backbone.js Model-View-Controller (MVC) framework can be used to make complex applications more manageable and easier to maintain.

If you felt comfortable with the previous Message Board with jQuery example, let's build upon it with the use of the Backbone.js framework. We will change the app to use Backbone but the look will remain moslty the same (see Figure 5-1).

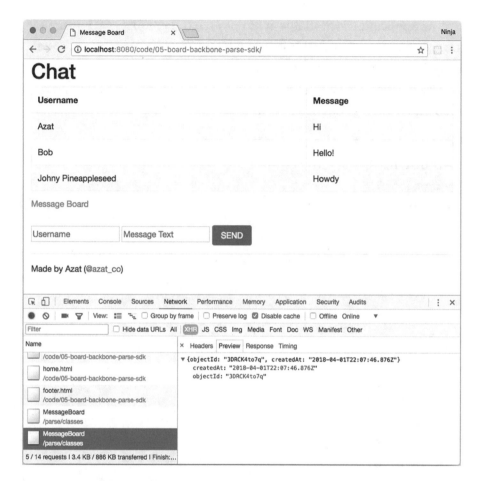

Figure 5-1. *Message Board powered by local Parse server*

Next we'll go step by step, creating a Message Board application using Backbone.js and Parse JavaScript SDK. If you feel familiar enough with it, you could download the Super Simple Backbone Starter Kit at `http://bit.ly/2LhjDE4`. Integration with Backbone.js will allow for a straightforward implementation of user actions by binding them to asynchronous updates of the collection.

The application is available at `http://bit.ly/2LfB9IQ`, but again you are encouraged to start from scratch and try to write your own code using the example only as a reference.

The following shows the structure of the Message Board with Parse, JavaScript SDK, and Backbone.js version:

```
/06-board-backbone-parse-sdk
  -index.html
  -home.html
  -footer.html
  -header.html
  -app.js
  /css
    -bootstrap.css
    -bootstrap.min.css
  /js
    -backbone.js
    -jquery.js
    -underscore.js
  /libs
    -require.min.js
    -text.js
```

Create a folder; in the folder create an `index.html` file with the following content skeleton:

```
<!DOCTYPE html>
<html lang="en">
  <head>
  ...
  </head>
```

```
<body>
  . . .
</body>
</html>
```

Download the necessary libraries or hot-link them from a CDN. Next include JavaScript libraries and Bootstrap stylesheets into the `<head>` element along with other important but not required *meta* elements.

```
<head>
  <meta charset="utf-8" />
  <title>Message Board</title>
  <meta name="author" content="Azat Mardan" />
```

We need this for responsive behavior:

```
<meta name="viewport"
  content="width=device-width, initial-scale=1.0" />
```

Link jQuery from a local file (v2.1.4 or higher):

```
<script src="js/jquery.js"></script>
```

Do the same for Underscore (v1.8.3 or higher) and Backbone (v1.2.3 or higher):

```
<script src="js/underscore.js"></script>
<script src="js/backbone.js"></script>
```

The Parse JavaScript SDK v1.5.0 is patched, meaning it's modified to work with the local Parse server. In this version, I commented or deleted the /1 in the URL path. The file is in the js folder of this project. Note this, because other versions might not work properly with this example:

```
<script src="js/parse-1.5.0.js"></script>
```

The Bootstrap CSS inclusion requires the following:

```
<link type="text/css" rel="stylesheet"
href="css/bootstrap.css" />
```

We need to have RequireJS (v2.1.22 or higher) for loading dependencies:

```
<script type="text/javascript" src="libs/require.js">
</script>
```

And here's our JS application inclusion:

```
<script type="text/javascript" src="app.js"></script>
</head>
```

Populate the <body> element with Bootstrap scaffolding (introduced in Chapter 1, "Basics"):

```
<body>
<div class="container-fluid">
  <div class="row-fluid">
    <div class="col-md-12">
      <div id="header">
      </div>
    </div>
  </div>
  <div class="row-fluid">
    <div class="col-md-12">
      <div id="content">
      </div>
    </div>
  </div>
```

```html
<div class="row-fluid">
  <div class="col-md-12">
    <div id="footer">
    </div>
  </div>
</div>
</div>
</body>
```

Create an `app.js` file and put Backbone.js views inside:

- `headerView`: Menu and app-common information

- `footerView`: Copyrights and contact links

- `homeView`: Home page content

We use Require.js syntax and the Shim plug-in for HTML templates:

```js
require([
'libs/text!header.html',
'libs/text!home.html',
'libs/text!footer.html'], function (
   headerTpl,
   homeTpl,
   footerTpl) {
```

The following code adds the application router with a single index route:

```js
const ApplicationRouter = Backbone.Router.extend({
  routes: {
    "": "home",
    "*actions": "home"
  },
```

Before we do anything else, we can initialize views that are going to be used across the app:

```
initialize: function() {
  this.headerView = new HeaderView()
  this.headerView.render()
  this.footerView = new FooterView()
  this.footerView.render()
},
```

This code takes care of the home route:

```
home: function() {
  this.homeView = new HomeView()
  this.homeView.render()
}
})
```

The header Backbone View is attached to the #header element and uses the headerTpl template:

```
HeaderView = Backbone.View.extend({
  el: '#header',
  templateFileName: 'header.html',
  template: headerTpl,
  initialize: function() {
  },
  render: function() {
    console.log(this.template)
    $(this.el).html(_.template(this.template))
  }
})
```

To render the HTML, we use the `jQuery.html()` function:

```
FooterView = Backbone.View.extend({
  el: '#footer',
  template: footerTpl,
  render: function() {
    this.$el.html(_.template(this.template))
  }
})
```

The home Backbone View definition uses the `#content` DOM element:

```
HomeView = Backbone.View.extend({
  el: '#content',
  template: homeTpl,
  initialize: function() {
  },
  render: function() {
    $(this.el).html(_.template(this.template))
  }
})
```

To start an app, we create a new instance and call `Backbone.history.start()`:

```
app = new ApplicationRouter()
  Backbone.history.start()
})
```

The full code of the `app.js` file is shown here:

```
require([
    'libs/text!header.html',
    // Example of a shim plugin use
    'libs/text!home.html',
    'libs/text!footer.html'],
  function (
    headerTpl,
    homeTpl,
    footerTpl) {
    const ApplicationRouter = Backbone.Router.extend({
      routes: {
        ' ': 'home',
        '*actions': 'home'
      },
      initialize: function() {
        this.headerView = new HeaderView()
        this.headerView.render()
        this.footerView = new FooterView()
        this.footerView.render()
      },
      home: function() {
        this.homeView = new HomeView()
        this.homeView.render()
      }
    })
  HeaderView = Backbone.View.extend({
    el: '#header',
    templateFileName: 'header.html',
    template: headerTpl,
    initialize: function() {
    },
```

```
  render: function() {
    console.log(this.template)
    $(this.el).html(_.template(this.template))
  }
})

FooterView = Backbone.View.extend({
  el: '#footer',
  template: footerTpl,
  render: function() {
    this.$el.html(_.template(this.template))
  }
})

HomeView = Backbone.View.extend({
  el: '#content',
  template: homeTpl,
  initialize: function() {
  },
  render: function() {
    $(this.el).html(_.template(this.template))
  }
})

app = new ApplicationRouter()
Backbone.history.start()
})
```

The code above displays templates. All views and routers are inside, requiring the module to make sure that the templates are loaded before we begin to process them.

Here is what `home.html` looks like:

- A table of messages

- Underscore.js logic to output rows of the table

- A new message form

Let's use the Bootstrap library structure (with its responsive components) by assigning `row-fluid` and `col-md-12` classes:

```
<div class="row-fluid" id="message-board">
<div class="col-md-12">
  <table class="table table-bordered table-striped">
    <caption>Message Board</caption>
    <thead>
      <tr>
        <th class="span2">Username</th>
        <th>Message</th>
      </tr>
    </thead>
    <tbody>
```

This part has Underscore.js template instructions, which are just some JS code wrapped in `<%` and `%>` marks. Right away we are checking that the `models` variable is defined and not empty:

```
<%
if (typeof models != 'undefined' &&
models.length > 0) {
```

`_.each()` is an iterator function from the UnderscoreJS TK library (`http://underscorejs.org/#each`), which does exactly what it sounds like—iterates through elements of an object/array:

```
_.each(models, function (value, key, list) { %>
  <tr>
```

198

Inside of the iterator function we have the argument `value` that is a single model from `models`. We can access attributes of the Backbone model with `model.attributes.attributeName`. To output variables in Underscore, we use `<%= NAME %>` instead of `<% CODE %>`:

```
      <td><%= value.attributes.username %></td>
      <td><%= value.attributes.message %></td>
    </tr>
  <% })
  }
```

But what if `models` is undefined or empty? In this case, we print a message that says that there's no messages yet. It goes into the `else` block. We use `colspan=2` to merge two cells into one:

```
  else { %>
  <tr>
    <td colspan="2">No messages yet</td>
  </tr>
```

We close the table and other HTML tags:

```
    <%}%>
    </tbody>
  </table>
</div>
</div>
```

For the new message form, we also use the `row-fluid` class and then add `<input>` elements:

```
<div class="row-fluid" id="new-message">
  <div class="col-md-12">
    <form class="well form-inline">
```

The `<input>` element must have the name `username` because that's how we find this element and get the username value in the JavaScript code:

```
<input type="text"
  name="username"
  class="input-small"
  placeholder="Username" />
```

Analogous to the username `<input>` tag, the message text tag needs to have the name. In this case, it's `message`:

```
<input type="text" name="message"
  class="input-small"
  placeholder="Message Text" />
```

Lastly, the "SEND" button must have the ID of `send`. This is what we use in the `events` property of the Backbone's `HomeView` class:

```
    <a id="send" class="btn btn-primary">SEND</a>
  </form>
  </div>
</div>
```

For your convenience, here's the full code of the `home.html` template file:

```
<div class="row-fluid" id="message-board">
<div class="col-md-12">
  <table class="table table-bordered table-striped">
    <caption>Message Board</caption>
    <thead>
      <tr>
        <th class="span2">Username</th>
        <th>Message</th>
      </tr>
    </thead>
```

```html
<tbody>
  <% if (typeof models != 'undefined' && models.
  length>0) {
    _.each(models, function (value,key, list) { %>
      <tr>
        <td><%= value.attributes.username %></td>
        <td><%= value.attributes.message %></td>
      </tr>
    <% })
  }
  else { %>
  <tr>
    <td colspan="2">No messages yet</td>
  </tr>
  <%}%>
</tbody>
  </table>
</div>
</div>
<div class="row-fluid" id="new-message">
  <div class="col-md-12">
    <form class="well form-inline">
      <input type="text"
        name="username"
        class="input-small"
        placeholder="Username" />
      <input type="text" name="message"
        class="input-small"
        placeholder="Message Text" />
```

```
        <a id="send" class-"btn btn-primary">SEND</a>
    </form>
  </div>
</div>
```

Now we can add the following components:

- Parse collection

- Parse model

- Send/add message event

- Getting/displaying messages functions

The following is a Backbone-compatible model/class `Parse.Object` from Parse JS SDK. It has a mandatory `className` attribute. This is the name of the collection. We define the model with `extend()`:

```
Message = Parse.Object.extend({
    className: 'MessageBoard'
})
```

Next is the Backbone-compatible collection class/object `Parse.Collection` from Parse JavaScript SDK that points to the just created `Message` model using the `model` property:

```
MessageBoard = Parse.Collection.extend ({
    model: Message
})
```

The `HomeView` object needs to have the `click` event listener on the "SEND" button:

```
HomeView = Backbone.View.extend({
    el: '#content',
    template: homeTpl,
```

```
events: {
    'click #send': 'saveMessage'
},
```

When we create `HomeView`, let's also create a collection and attach event listeners to it:

```
initialize: function() {
    this.collection = new MessageBoard()
    this.collection.bind('all', this.render, this)
    this.collection.fetch()
    this.collection.on('add', function(message) {
        message.save(null, {
            success: function(message) {
                console.log('saved ' + message)
            },
            error: function(message) {
                console.log('error')
            }
        })
        console.log('saved' + message)
    })
},
```

Next is the definition of `saveMessage()` calls for the "SEND" button `click` event that goes on the same `HomeView` object as a property:

```
saveMessage: function() {
```

Firstly, we get the form object by its ID (`#new-message`) because it's more effective and readable to use a stored object rather than use jQuery selector every time.

```
const newMessageForm = $('#new-message')
```

The next two lines will get the values of the input fields with names `username` and `message`:

```
const username = newMessageForm.
find('[name="username"]').val()
const message = newMessageForm.
find('[name="message"]').val()
```

Once we have the values of a new message (text and author), we can invoke `this.collection.add()`:

```
this.collection.add({
  'username': username,
  'message': message
})
},
```

Last, we output the collections by using `_.template` with the template from `this.template`, and then invoking it with the data coming from `this.collection`:

```
render: function() {
    $(this.el).html(_.template(this.template)
(this.collection))
}
```

The end result of our manipulations in `app.js` might look something like this:

```
require([
  'libs/text!header.html',
  'libs/text!home.html',
  'libs/text!footer.html'], function (
    headerTpl,
```

```
        homeTpl,
        footerTpl) {

    Parse.initialize('your-parse-app-id',
'your-parse-js-sdk-key')

    const ApplicationRouter = Backbone.Router.extend({
        routes: {
            ' ': 'home',
            '*actions': 'home'
        },
        initialize: function() {
            this.headerView = new HeaderView()
            this.headerView.render()
            this.footerView = new FooterView()
            this.footerView.render()
        },
        home: function() {
            this.homeView = new HomeView()
            this.homeView.render()
        }
    })

    HeaderView = Backbone.View.extend ({
        el: '#header',
        templateFileName: 'header.html',
        template: headerTpl,
        initialize: function() {
        },
        render: function() {
            $(this.el).html(_.template(this.template))
        }
    })
```

```
FooterView = Backbone.View.extend({
    el: '#footer',
    template: footerTpl,
    render: function() {
        this.$el.html(_.template(this.template))
    }
})
Message = Parse.Object.extend({
    className: 'MessageBoard'
})
MessageBoard = Parse.Collection.extend ({
    model: Message
})

HomeView = Backbone.View.extend({
    el: '#content',
    template: homeTpl,
    events: {
        'click #send': 'saveMessage'
    },

    initialize: function(){
        this.collection = new MessageBoard()
        this.collection.bind('all', this.render, this)
        this.collection.fetch()
        this.collection.on('add', function(message) {
            message.save(null, {
                success: function(message) {
                    console.log('saved ' + message)
                },
```

```
                    error: function(message) {
                        console.log('error')
                    }
                })
                console.log('saved' + message)
            })
        },
        saveMessage: function(){
            const newMessageForm = $('#new-message')
            const username = newMessageForm.
find('[name="username"]').val()
            const message = newMessageForm.
find('[name="message"]').val()
            this.collection.add({
                'username': username,
                'message': message
            })
        },
        render: function() {
          $(this.el).html(_.template(this.template)(this.
collection))
        }
    })

    window.app = new ApplicationRouter ()
    Backbone.history.start()
})
```

Again, the full source code of the Backbone.js and Parse Message Board application is available at http://bit.ly/2LfB9IQ.

Taking Message Board Further

Once you are comfortable that your front-end application works well locally, with or without a local HTTP server like MAMP or XAMPP, deploy it to Microsoft Azure or Heroku. In-depth deployment instructions are described in Chapter 1, "Getting Data from Backend Using jQuery and Parse".

In the last two examples, Message Board had very basic functionality. You could enhance the application by adding more features.

I created a list of additional features for *intermediate* level developers to implement as an exercise:

- Sort the list of messages through the `updateAt` attribute before displaying it.

- Add a "Refresh" button to update the list of messages.

- Save the username after the first message entry in a runtime memory or in a session.

- Add an up-vote button next to each message, and store the votes.

- Add a down-vote button next to each message, and store the votes.

Here are a few recommended additional features for *advanced* level developers:

- Add a User collection.

- Prevent the same user from voting multiple times.

- Add user sign-up and log-in actions by using Parse functions.

- Add a "Delete Message" button next to each message created by a user.

- Add an "Edit Message" button next to each message created by a user.

Summary

This short chapter gives you yet another way of building apps with nothing but JavaScript (and HTML and CSS, obviously). With Parse or a similar back-end-as-a-service (BaaS) solution, it is straightforward to persist the data without having to code your own backend. BaaS solutions take it a step further by allowing for access-level controls, authentications, server-side logic, and third-party integrations.

In addition to leveraging Parse in this chapter, we saw how Backbone can be flexible in terms of allowing you to overload its classes to build your own custom ones. This is a way to use Backbone to build your own framework. This is what we did at DocuSign when I worked there; we had base Backbone models and extended them for custom use cases. We even shared Backbone models between the server and the browser, allowing for faster data loading. Speaking of the server JavaScript, in the next chapter we'll explore how to write JavaScript on the server with Node.js.

PART III

Back-End Prototyping

CHAPTER 6

Intro to Node.js

Any fool can write code that a computer can understand.
Good programmers write code that humans can understand.

—Martin Fowler

In this chapter, we'll cover the following:

- Building "Hello World" in Node.js

- Node.js core modules

- npm Node.js package manager

- Message Board with Node.js: memory store version

- Unit testing Node.js

Node.js is a non-blocking platform for building web applications. It uses JavaScript, so it's a centerpiece in our full stack JavaScript development. We'll start by building our "Hello World" app and then we'll cover core modules and npm. Then, we deploy our "Hello World" app to the cloud.

© Azat Mardan 2018
A. Mardan, *Full Stack JavaScript*, https://doi.org/10.1007/978-1-4842-3718-2_6

Building "Hello World" in Node.js

To check if you have Node.js installed on your computer, type and execute this command in your terminal:

```
$ node -v
```

Get the version 8 or higher. If you don't have Node.js installed, or if your version is older (behind or lower), you can download the latest version at `http://nodejs.org/#download`. You can use one of these tools for version management (i.e., switching between Node.js versions):

- n: `https://npmjs.com/n`

- nave: `https://npmjs.com/nave`

- nvm: `https://npmjs.com/nvm`

- nvm-windows: `https://github.com/coreybutler/nvm-windows`

As usual, you could copy the example code at `http://bit.ly/2Lbvxzr`, or write your own program from scratch. If you wish to do the latter, create a folder `hello` for your "Hello World" Node.js application. Then create a file `server.js` and line by line type the code below.

This line will load the core `http` module for the server (more on the modules later):

```
const http = require('http')
```

We'll need a port number for our Node.js server. To get it from the environment or assign 1337 if the environment is not set, use:

```
const port = process.env.PORT || 1337
```

This will create a server, and a callback function will contain the response handler code:

```
const server = http.createServer((req, res) => {
```

214

To set the right header and status code, use:

```
res.writeHead(200, {'Content-Type': 'text/plain'})
```

To output "Hello World" with the line end symbol, use:

```
res.end('Hello World\n')
})
```

To set a port and display the address of the server and the port number, use:

```
server.listen(port, () => {
  console.log('Server is running at %s:%s ',
    server.address().address, server.address().port)
})
```

From the folder in which you have `server.js`, launch in your terminal the following command:

```
$ node server.js
```

Open http://localhost:1337 or http://127.0.0.1:1337 or any other address you see in the terminal as a result of the `console.log()` function, and you should see "Hello World" in a browser. To shut down the server, press Control + C.

Note   The name of the main file could be different from `server.js` (e.g., `index.js` or `app.js`). In case you need to launch the `app.js` file, just use `$ node app.js`.

Node.js Core Modules

Unlike other programming technologies, Node.js doesn't come with a heavy standard library. The core modules of Node.js are a bare minimum and the rest can be cherry-picked via the npm Node.js package manager registry. The main core modules, classes, methods, and events include:

- http (`https://nodejs.org/api/http.html`): Module for working with HTTP protocol

- util (`https://nodejs.org/api/util.html`): Module with various helpers

- querystring (`https://nodejs.org/api/querystring.html`): Module for parsing query strings from the URI

- url (`https://nodejs.org/api/url.html`): Module for parsing URI information

- fs (`https://nodejs.org/api/fs.html`): Module for working with the file system

These are the most important core modules. Let's take a look at each of them.

http

This is the main module responsible for the Node.js HTTP server. Here are the main methods:

- `http.createServer()`: Returns a new web server object

- `http.listen()`: Begins accepting connections on the specified port and hostname

- `http.ServerRequest()`: Passes incoming requests to request handlers

  - `data`: Emitted when a piece of the message body is received

  - `end`: Emitted exactly once for each request

  - `request.method()`: The request method as a string

  - `request.url()`: Request URL string

- `http.ServerResponse()`: Provides response/output of request handlers initiated by an HTTP server—not by the user

  - `response.writeHead()`: Sends a response header to the request

  - `response.write()`: Sends a response body

  - `response.end()`: Sends and ends a response body

util

This module provides a utility for debugging:

- `util.inspect()`: Returns a string representation of an object, which is useful for debugging

querystring

This module provides utilities for dealing with query strings. Some of the methods include:

- `querystring.stringify()`: Serializes an object to a query string

- `querystring.parse()`: Deserializes a query string to an object

url

This module has a utility for URL resolution and parsing:

- `url.parse()`: Takes a URL string, and returns an object which has URL information broken down into parts

fs

`fs` handles file system operations such as reading and writing to/from files. There are synchronous and asynchronous methods in the library. Some of the methods include:

- `fs.readFile()`: Reads file asynchronously

- `fs.writeFile()`: Writes data to file asynchronously

There is no need to install or download core modules. To include them in your application, all you need is to follow the syntax:

```
const http = require('http')
```

The lists of non-core modules can be found at:

- npmjs.org: Node.js Package Manager registry

- Nipster (`http://eirikb.github.io/nipster`): npm search tool for Node.js

- node-modules (`http://node-modules.com`): npm search engine

If you would like to know how to code your own modules, take a look at Chapter 12 "Modularizing Your Code and Publishing Node.js Modules to npm" of Practical Node.js, 2nd Edition: `http://bit.ly/2LkG0Zk`.

npm Node.js Package Manager

Node.js Package Manager, or npm, manages dependencies and installs modules for you. Node.js installation comes with npm, whose web site is npmjs.org.

`package.json` contains meta information about our Node.js application such as a version number; author name; and, most important, what dependencies we use in the application. All of that information is in the JSON formatted object, which is read by npm.

If you would like to install packages and dependencies specified in `package.json`, type:

```
$ npm install
```

A typical `package.json` file might look like this:

```
{
    "name": "Blerg",
    "description": "Blerg blerg blerg.",
    "version": "0.0.1",
    "author": {
```

```
        "name" : "John Doe",
        "email" : "john.doe@gmail.com"
    },
    "repository": {
        "type": "git",
        "url": "http://github.com/johndoe/blerg.git"
    },
    "engines": [
        "node >= 0.6.2"
    ],
    "scripts": {
        "start": "server.js"
    },
    "license" : "MIT",
    "dependencies": {
        "express": ">= 2.5.6",
        "mustache": "0.4.0",
        "commander": "0.5.2"
    },
    "bin" : {
        "blerg" : "./cli.js"
    }
}
```

While most of the properties in the `package.json` example above like `description` and `name` are self-explanatory, others deserve more explaining. The `dependencies` property is an object, and each item has the name on the left side and the version number on the right side. For example, this statement tells npm to use Express.js version 2.5.6 or lower (earlier):

```
"express": "<= 2.5.6"
```

The version can be exact (recommended). For example, this statement locks the version of Express.js at 2.5.6.:

```
"express": "2.5.6,"
```

The versions can be specified to be greater-than (>), less-than (<), or any/wildcard (*). For example, this statement tell npm to use any version which usually means npm will get the latest stable version:

```
"express": "*"
```

A wild card is a great way to blow up your app in production with new untested dependencies: therefore not recommended.

The `bin` property is for command-line utilities. It tells the system what file to launch. And the `scripts` object has scripts that you can launch with `$ npm run SCRIPT_NAME`. The `start` and `test` scripts are exceptions. You can run them with `$ npm start` and `$ npm test`.

To update a package to its current latest version or the latest version that is allowable by the version specification defined in `package.json`, use:

```
$ npm update name-of-the-package
```

Or for single module installation:

```
$ npm install name-of-the-package
```

The only module used in this book's examples—and which does not belong to the core Node.js package—is `mongodb`. We'll install it in the next chapter.

However, Heroku will need `package.json` to run npm on the server. The easiest way to create `package.json` is to execute:

```
$ npm init -y
```

Deploying "Hello World" to PaaS

For Heroku and Microsoft Azure deployment, we'll need a Git repository. To create it from the root of your project, type the following command in your terminal:

```
$ git init
```

Git will create a hidden `.git` folder. Now we can add files and make the first commit:

```
$ git add .
$ git commit -am "first commit"
```

Tip To view hidden files on the macOS Finder app, execute this command in a terminal window:

```
defaults write com.apple.finder AppleShowAllFiles -bool true
```

To change the flag back to hidden:

```
defaults write com.apple.finder AppleShowAllFiles -bool false
```

Deploying to Microsoft Azure

In order to deploy our "Hello World" application to Microsoft Azure, we must add a Git remote destination that belongs to Azure. You could copy the URI/URL from the Microsoft Azure Portal, and use it with this command:

```
$ git remote add azure YOUR_AZURE_URI
```

Now we should be able to make a push with this command:

```
$ git push azure master
```

If everything went okay, you should see success logs in the terminal and "Hello World" in the browser of your Microsoft Azure Web Site URL.

To push changes, just execute:

```
$ git add .
$ git commit -m "changing to hello azure"
$ git push azure master
```

A more meticulous guide can be found in the tutorial `http://bit.ly/2LbXQOi`.

Deploying to Heroku

For Heroku deployment, we need to create two extra files: `Procfile` and `package.json`. You could get the source code from `http://bit.ly/2Lbvxzr` or write your own one.

The structure of the "Hello World" application looks like this:

```
/06-hello
  -package.json
  -Procfile
  -server.js
```

`Procfile` is a mechanism for declaring what commands are run by your application's dynos on the Heroku platform. Basically, it tells Heroku what processes to run. `Procfile` has only one line in this case:

```
web: node server.js
```

For this example, we keep `package.json` simple:

```
{
  "name": "node-example",
  "version": "0.0.1",
  "dependencies": {
  },
  "engines": {
    "node": ">=0.6.x"
  }
}
```

After we have all of the files in the project folder, we can use Git to deploy the application. The commands are pretty much the same as with Microsoft Azure except that we need to add Git remote, and create Cedar Stack with:

```
$ heroku create
```

After it's done, we push and update with:

```
$ git push heroku master
$ git add .
$ git commit -am "changes :+1:"
$ git push heroku master
```

If everything went okay, you should see success logs in the terminal and "Hello World" in the browser of your Heroku app URL.

Message Board with Node.js: Memory Store Version

The first version of the Message Board back-end application will store messages only in runtime memory storage for the sake of the KISS principle—keep it simple stupid (http://azat.co/blog/kiss). That means that each time we start/reset the server, the data will be lost.

We'll start with a simple test case first to illustrate the Test-Driven Development approach. The full code is available at the book's GitHub repository in the code/06-test folder: http://bit.ly/2LcnHWv.

Unit Testing Node.js

We should have two methods:

1. Get all of the messages as an array of JSON objects for the GET /message endpoint using the getMessages() method

2. Add a new message with properties name and message for the POST /messages route via the addMessage() function

We'll start by creating an empty mb-server.js file. After it's there, let's switch to tests and create the test.js file with the following content:

```
const http = require('http')
const assert = require('assert')
const querystring = require('querystring')
const util = require('util')

const messageBoard = require('./mb-server')

assert.deepEqual('[{"name":"John","message":"hi"}]',
  messageBoard.getMessages())
```

225

```
assert.deepEqual ('{"name":"Jake","message":"gogo"}',
  messageBoard.addMessage ("name=Jake&message=gogo"))
assert.deepEqual('[{"name":"John","message":"hi"},{"name":
"Jake","message":"gogo"}]',
  messageBoard.getMessages())
```

Please keep in mind that this is a very simplified comparison of strings and not JavaScript objects. So every space, quote, and case matters. You could make the comparison "smarter" by parsing a string into a JSON object with:

```
JSON.parse(str)
```

For testing our assumptions, we use the core Node.js module assert. It provides a bunch of useful methods like `equal()`, `deepEqual()`, etc.

More advanced libraries include alternative interfaces with TDD and/or BDD approaches:

- `expect.js` (`https://www.npmjs.com/expect.js`): Minimalistic BDD-style assertion library: for example, `expect(user.name).to.eql('azat')`

- `should` (`https://www.npmjs.com/should` and `http://shouldjs.github.io`): BDD-style assertion library that works by modifying `Object.prototype`: for example, `user.name.should.be.eql('azat')`

For more Test-Driven Development and cutting-edge automated testing, you could use the following libraries and modules:

- `mocha` (`https://www.npmjs.com/mocha` and `https://mochajs.org`): Feature-rich testing framework (my default choice)

- `jasmine` (`https://www.npmjs.com/jasmine` `https://jasmine.github.io`): BDD testing framework with built-in assertion and spy (for mocking) libraries

- vows (`https://www.npmjs.com/vows` and `http://vowsjs.org`): BDD framework for Node.js tailored to testing asynchronous code

- chai (`https://www.npmjs.com/chaijs` and `http://chaijs.com`): BDD/TDD assertion library that can be paired with a testing framework and has its own versions of Should, Expect, and Assert

- tape (`https://www.npmjs.com/tape`): A minimalistic TAP (Test Anything Protocol) library

- jest (`https://www.npmjs.com/jest` and `https://jestjs.io`): Jasmine-and-Expect-like testing library with automatic mocks

You could copy the "Hello World" script into the `mb-server.js` file for now or even keep it empty. If we run `test.js` by the terminal command:

```
$ node test.js
```

we should see an error, probably something like this one:

```
TypeError: Object #<Object> has no method 'getMessages'
```

That's totally fine, because we haven't written the `getMessages()` method yet. So let's do it and make our application more useful by adding two new methods: to get the list of the messages for Chat and to add a new message to the collection.

Here's the `mb-server.js` file with the global `exports` object:

```
exports.getMessages = function() {
    return JSON.stringify(messages)
    // Output array of messages as a string/text
}
```

227

```
exports.addMessage = function (data){
    messages.push(querystring.parse(data))
    // To convert string into JavaScript object we use
    parse/deserializer
    return JSON.stringify(querystring.parse(data))
    // Output new message in JSON as a string
}
```

We import dependencies:

```
const http = require('http')
// Loads http module
const util= require('util')
// Usefull functions
const querystring = require('querystring')
// Loads querystring module, we'll need it to serialize
and deserialize objects and query strings
```

And set the port. If it's set in the environment variable PORT (e.g., $ PORT=3000 node server.js), we use that value; and if it's not set, we use a hard-coded value of 1337:

```
const port = process.env.PORT || 1337
```

So far, nothing fancy, right? To store the list of messages, we'll use an array:

```
const messages=[]
// This array will hold our messages
messages.push({
    'name': 'John',
    'message': 'hi'
})
// Sample message to test list method
```

Generally, fixtures like dummy data belong to the test/spec files and not to the main application code base.

Our server code will look slightly more interesting. For getting the list of messages, according to REST methodology, we need to make a GET request. For creating/adding a new message, it should be a POST request. So in our `createServer` object, we should add `req.method()` and `req.url()` to check for an HTTP request type and a URL path.

Let's load the `http` module:

```
const http = require('http')
```

We'll need some of the handy functions from the `util` and `querystring` modules (to serialize and deserialize objects and query strings):

```
const util= require('util')
// Usefull functions
const querystring = require('querystring')
// Loads querystring module, we'll need it to serialize
and deserialize objects and query strings
```

To create a server and expose it to outside modules (i.e., `test.js`):

```
exports.server=http.createServer(function (req, res) {
// Creates server
```

Inside of the request handler callback, we should check if the request method is POST and the URL is `messages/create.json`:

```
if (req.method == 'POST' && req.url == '/messages/
   create.json') {
  // If method is POST and URL is messages/ add message
     to the array
```

If the condition above is true, we add a message to the array. However, `data` must be converted to a string type (with encoding UTF–8) prior to the adding, because it is a type of `Buffer`:

```
let message = ''
req.on('data', function(data, msg) {
    console.log(data.toString('utf-8'))
    message=exports.addMessage(data.toString('utf-8'))
    // Data is type of Buffer and must be converted to
       string with encoding UTF-8 first
    // Adds message to the array
})
```

These logs will help us to monitor the server activity in the terminal:

```
req.on('end', function() {
    console.log('message', util.inspect(message, true,
    null))
    console.log('messages:', util.inspect(messages,
    true, null))
    // Debugging output into the terminal
```

The output should be in a text format with a status of 200 (okay):

```
res.writeHead(200, {'Content-Type': 'text/plain'})
    // Sets the right header and status code
```

We output a message with a newly created object ID:

```
res.end(message)
    // Output message, should add object id
  })
```

If the method is GET and the URL is `/messages/list.json`, output a list of messages:

```
} else if (req.method == 'GET' && req.url == '/messages/
list.json') {
// If method is GET and URL is /messages output list of
messages
```

Fetch a list of messages:

```
const body = exports.getMessages()
// Body will hold our output
```

The response body will hold our output:

```
res.writeHead(200, {
  'Content-Length': body.length,
  'Content-Type': 'text/plain'
})
res.end(body)
```

The next `else` is for when there's not a match for any of the previous conditions. This sets the right header and status code:

```
} else {
res.writeHead(200, {'Content-Type': 'text/plain'})
// Sets the right header and status code
```

In case it's neither of the two endpoints above, we output a string with a line end symbol:

```
res.end('Hello World\n')
// Outputs string with line end symbol
}
```

Start the server:

```
}).listen(port)
// Sets port and IP address of the server
```

Now, we should set a port and IP address of the server:

```
console.log('Server running at http://127.0.0.1:%s/', port)
```

We expose methods for the unit testing in `test.js` (`exports` keyword), and this function returns an array of messages as a string/text:

```
exports.getMessages = function() {
  return JSON.stringify(messages)
}
```

`addMessage()` converts a string into a JavaScript object with the `parse()` deserializer method from `querystring`:

```
exports.addMessage = function (data) {
  messages.push(querystring.parse(data))
```

We also return a new message in a JSON-as-a-string format:

```
  return JSON.stringify(querystring.parse(data))
}
```

Here is the full code of `mb-server.js` minus the comments. It's also available in the code/06-test folder.

```
const http = require('http')
// Loads http module
const util= require('util')
// Usefull functions
const querystring = require('querystring')
// Loads querystring module, we'll need it to serialize
and deserialize objects and query strings
```

```
const port = process.env.PORT || 1337

const messages=[]
// This array will hold our messages
messages.push({
  'name': 'John',
  'message': 'hi'
})
// Sample message to test list method
exports.server=http.createServer(function (req, res) {
// Creates server
  if (req.method == 'POST' && req.url == '/messages/
  create.json') {
    // If method is POST and URL is messages/ add message
    to the array
    let message = "
    req.on('data', function(data, msg) {
      console.log(data.toString('utf-8'))
      message=exports.addMessage(data.toString('utf-8'))
      // Data is type of Buffer and must be converted to
      string with encoding UTF-8 first
      // Adds message to the array
    })
    req.on('end', function() {
      console.log('message', util.inspect(message, true,
      null))
      console.log('messages:', util.inspect(messages,
      true, null))
      // Debugging output into the terminal
      res.writeHead(200, {'Content-Type': 'text/plain'})
      // Sets the right header and status code
      res.end(message)
```

```
      // Output message, should add object id
    })
  } else
  if (req.method == 'GET' && req.url == '/messages/list.
json') {
  // If method is GET and URL is /messages output list of
  messages
    const body = exports.getMessages()
    // Body will hold our output
    res.writeHead(200, {
      'Content-Length': body.length,
      'Content-Type': 'text/plain'
    })
    res.end(body)
  } else {
    res.writeHead(200, {'Content-Type': 'text/plain'})
    // Sets the right header and status code
    res.end('Hello World\n')
    // Outputs string with line end symbol
  }

}).listen(port)
// Sets port and IP address of the server
console.log('Server running at http://127.0.0.1:%s/', port)

exports.getMessages = function() {
  return JSON.stringify(messages)
  // Output array of messages as a string/text
}
exports.addMessage = function (data) {
  messages.push(querystring.parse(data))
```

```
// To convert string into JavaScript object we use
parse/deserializer
return JSON.stringify(querystring.parse(data))
// Output new message in JSON as a string
}
```

To check it, go to http://localhost:1337/messages/list.json. You should see an example message. Alternatively, you could use the terminal command to fetch the messages:

```
$ curl http://127.0.0.1:1337/messages/list.json
```

To make the POST request by using a command-line interface:

```
$ curl -d "name=BOB&message=test" http://127.0.0.1:1337/
messages/create.json
```

And you should get the output in a server terminal window and a new message "test" when you refresh http://localhost:1337/messages/list.json. Needless to say, all three tests should pass.

Your application might grow bigger with more methods, URL paths to parse, and conditions. That is where frameworks come in handy. They provide helpers to process requests and other nice things like static file support, sessions, etc. In this example, we intentionally didn't use any frameworks like Express.js or Restify but there are many powerful and useful frameworks for Node. Here's the list of the most popular and notable Node.js frameworks:

- Derby (http://derbyjs.com): MVC framework makes it easy to write real-time, collaborative applications that run in both Node.js and browsers

- Express.js (http://expressjs.com): The most robust, tested and used Node.js framework

- Restify (`http://restify.com`): Lightweight framework for REST API servers

- Sails (`http://sailsjs.org`): MVC Node.js framework with rich scaffolding

- hapi (`https://hapijs.com`): Node.js framework built on top of Express.js

- Connect (`https://github.com/senchalabs/connect`): Middleware framework for Node.js, shipping with over 18 bundled middlewares and a rich selection of third-party middleware

- GeddyJS (`http://geddyjs.org`): Simple, structured MVC web framework for Node.js

- CompoundJS (`http://compoundjs.com`) (exRailswayJS): Node.js MVC framework based on Express.js

- Tower.js (`http://tower.github.io`): Full stack web framework for Node.js and the browser

- Meteor (`https://www.meteor.com`): Open source platform for building top-quality web apps in a fraction of the time

For a list of hand-picked Node.js frameworks, take a look at `http://nodeframeworks.com`.

Next, I will explain a few ways to improve the REST API application. These are your assignments to give you more practice and make the learning more effective:

- Improve existing test cases by adding object comparison instead of a string one

- Move the seed data to `test.js` from `mb-server.js`

- Add test cases to support your frontend (e.g., up vote, user login)

- Add methods to support your frontend (e.g., up-vote, user login)

- Generate unique IDs for each message and store them in a Hash instead of an Array

- Install Mocha and refactor `test.js` so it uses this library

So far we've been storing our messages in the application memory, so each time the application is restarted, we lose our messages. To fix it, we need to add persistence (more permanent store), and one of the best ways is to use a database like MongoDB, introduced in the next chapter.

Summary

In this chapter we've covered important topics that will lay the foundation for all of your future Node.js development. This chapter taught the "Hello World" application in Node.js, listed of some of its most important Node.js core modules, explained the npm workflow, covered test-driven development practice, and provided detailed commands for deployment of Node.js apps to the Heroku and Microsoft Azure cloud services.

CHAPTER 7

Intro to MongoDB

What is Oracle? A bunch of people. And all of our products were just ideas in the heads of those people - ideas that people typed into a computer, tested, and that turned out to be the best idea for a database or for a programming language.

—Larry Ellison

In this chapter, we'll explore the following topics:

- MongoDB shell

- MongoDB Native Node.js Driver

- MongoDB on Heroku with MongoLab

- Message Board: MongoDB version

MongoDB is a NoSQL document-store database. It is scalable and performant. It has no schema so all the logic and relationships are implemented in the application layer. You can use object-document mappers (ODMs) like Waterline or Mongoose for that schema, validation and business logic implementation in Node.js.

What's good about MongoDB in addition to its scaling and performance is that MongoDB uses a JavaScript interface, which completes the full stack JavaScript stack puzzle of browser, server, and the database layers. With MongoDB we can use one language for all three layers. The easiest way to get started with MongoDB is to use its shell, a.k.a. REPL (read-eval-print-loop).

© Azat Mardan 2018
A. Mardan, *Full Stack JavaScript*, https://doi.org/10.1007/978-1-4842-3718-2_7

MongoDB Shell

If you haven't done so already, please install the latest version of MongoDB from `https://www.mongodb.com/download-center`. For more instructions, please refer to the "Database: MongoDB" section in Chapter 2. You might have to create a data folder per the instructions.

Now from the folder where you unpacked the archive, launch the `mongod` service with:

```
$ ./bin/mongod
```

You should be able to see information in your terminal and in the browser at localhost:28017.

For the MongoDB shell, or `mongo`, launch in a new terminal window (**important!**) and at the same folder this command:

```
$ ./bin/mongo
```

You should see something like this, depending on your version of the MongoDB shell (`$ mongo -version` or after `$ mongo`):

```
MongoDB shell version: 3.0.6
connecting to: test
```

To test the database, use the JavaScript-like interface and commands `save` and `find`:

```
> db.test.save( { a: 1 } )
> db.test.find()
```

Again, more detailed step-by-step instructions are available in the "Database: MongoDB" section of Chapter 2.

The following are some other useful MongoDB shell commands, which I've referenced in a MongoDB and Mongoose cheatsheet that you can download in PDF for free at `https://gum.co/mongodb/git-874e6fb4`

240

or view online at `http://bit.ly/2LatWtP`. Here's the short version of the reference:

- `> show dbs`: Show databases on the server

- `> use DB_NAME`: Select database `DB_NAME`

- `> show collections`: Show collections in the selected database

- `> db.COLLECTION_NAME.find()`: Perform the find query on collection with the `COLLECTION_NAME` name to find any items

- `> db.COLLECTION_NAME.find({"_id": ObjectId ("549d9a3081d0f07866fdaac6")})`: Perform the find query on collection with the `COLLECTION_NAME` name to find item with ID `549d9a3081d0f07866fdaac6`

- `> db.COLLECTION_NAME.find({"email": / gmail/})`: Perform the find query on collection with the `COLLECTION_NAME` name to find items with e-mail property matching `/gmail/` regular expression, e.g., bob@gmail.com or john@gmail.in

- `> db.COLLECTION_NAME.update(QUERY_OBJECT, SET_OBJECT)`: Perform the update query on collection with the `COLLECTION_NAME` name to update items that match `QUERY_OBJECT` with `SET_OBJECT`

- `> db.COLLECTION_NAME.remove(QUERY_OBJECT)`: Perform remove query for items matching `QUERY_OBJECT` criteria on the `COLLECTION_NAME` collection

- `> db.COLLECTION_NAME.insert(OBJECT)`: Add `OBJECT` to the collection with the `COLLECTION_NAME` name

So starting from a fresh shell session, you can execute these commands to create a document, change it, and remove it:

```
> help
> show dbs
> use board
> show collections
> db.messages.remove();
> var a = db.messages.findOne();
> printjson(a);
> a.message = "hi";
> a.name = "John";
> db.messages.save(a);
> db.messages.find({});
> db.messages.update({name: "John"},{$set: {message: "bye"}});
> db.messages.find({name: "John"});
> db.messages.remove({name: "John"});
```

MongoDB uses a special data format called BSON that has special types and one of them is Object ID. Let's cover it briefly next.

BSON Object ID

Binary JSON, or BSON, is a special data type that MongoDB utilizes. It is like JSON in notation but has support for additional, more sophisticated data types such as buffer or date.

A word of caution about BSON's Object ID: `ObjectId` in MongoDB shell and many other MongoDB driver is an equivalent to `ObjectID` in MongoDB Native Node.js Driver. Make sure to use the proper case and don't confuse the two, otherwise you'll get an error.

For example, in a Node.js code with the native driver use `ObjectID()`:

```
const mongodb = require('mongodb')
const ObjectID = mongodb.ObjectID
collection.findOne({_id: new ObjectID(idString)}, console.log)
```

On the other hand, in the MongoDB shell and many other MongoDB libraries like Mongoose, we employ `ObjectId()`. The following is the MongoDB shell code:

```
db.messages.findOne({_id: ObjectId(idStr)});
```

The following is a Node.js code with Mongoose:

```
const mongoose = require('mongoose')
const ObjectId = mongoose.Schema.Types.ObjectId
const Car = new Schema({ driver: ObjectId })
```

Note   Mongoose is a very powerful library for Node.js and MongoDB. It has validation, pre and post hooks, schemas and many more features. I wrote a whole chapter on Mongoose in my new book *Practical Node.js, 2nd Edition* (Apress, 2018). Get and read my book to learn more about Mongoose at: `http://bit.ly/2LdCNL3` and `https://github.com/azat-co/practicalnode`.

MongoDB Native Driver

We'll use MongoDB Native Node.js Driver (`https://github.com/christkv/node-mongodb-native`) to access MongoDB from Node.js applications. This will add persistence to Node.js apps meaning apps will save and retrieve data from a permanent location instead of relying on an ephemeral in-memory store. To install MongoDB Native Node.js Driver, use:

```
$ npm install mongodb
```

Keep in mind that the preceding command is to install the driver library, not the database. I taught many workshops and in almost every one of them there would be a person who would confuse installing `mongodb` using npm with installing a database. Don't be this person. We need both, the database and the npm library. I already covered the database installation. If you have any issue with installing the driver, read the details are at `https://mongodb.github.io/node-mongodb-native`.

Don't forget to include the dependency in the `package.json` file as well, either with `-SE` or manually, so that you have the file resembling this:

```
{
  "name": "node-example",
  "version": "0.0.1",
  "dependencies": {
    "mongodb":"3.x",

    ...
  },
  "engines": {
    "node": ">=8.x"
  }
}
```

Alternatively, for your own development you could use other mappers, which are available as an extension of the Native Driver:

- `mongoskin` (`https://npmjs.org/node-mongoskin`): Future layer for `node-mongodb-native`

- `mongoose` (`https://npmjs.org/mongoose` and `http://mongoosejs.com`): Asynchronous JavaScript driver with optional support for modeling

- mongolia (https://npmjs.org/mongolia):
  Lightweight MongoDB ORM/driver wrapper

- monk (https://npmjs.org/monk): Tiny layer that
  provides simple yet substantial usability improvements
  for MongoDB usage within Node.js

This small example will test if we can connect to a local MongoDB instance from a Node.js script. Create a Node.js file app.js. After we install the library with npm, we can include the mongodb library in our app.js file:

```
const util = require('util')
const mongodb = require ('mongodb')
```

This is one of the ways to establish a connection to the MongoDB server in which the db variable will hold a reference to the database at a specified host and port:

```
const Db = mongodb.Db
const Connection = mongodb.Connection
const Server = mongodb.Server
const host = '127.0.0.1'
const port = 27017

const db = new Db ('test', new Server(host,port, {}))
```

To actually open a connection:

```
db.open((error, connection) => {
  // Do something with the database here
  db.close()
})
```

To check that we have the connection, we need to handle `error`. Also, let's get the admin object with `db.admin()` and fetch the list of databases with `listDatabases()`:

```
const db = new Db ('test', new Server(host, port, {}))
db.open((error, connection) => {
  console.log('error: ', error)
  const adminDb = db.admin()
  adminDb.listDatabases((error, dbs) => {
    console.log('error: ', error)
    console.log('databases: ', dbs.databases)
    db.close()
  })
})
```

If we run it with `$ node app.js`, it should output "connected" in the terminal. When you're in doubt and need to check the properties of an object, there is a useful method in the `util` module:

```
console.log(util.inspect(db))
```

Now you might want to set up the database in the cloud and test the connection from your Node.js script.

MongoDB on Heroku: MongoLab

Now that you've made the application that displays "connected" work locally, it's time to slightly modify it and deploy it to the Heroku PaaS (cloud). The database will also be in the cloud. I recommend using the MongoLab add-on, which provides ready-to-use MongoDB instances that integrate well with Heroku apps (`https://elements.heroku.com/addons/mongolab`). MongoLab (or mLab) also has a very convenient browser- based GUI to look up and manipulate the data and collections.

Note   You might have to provide your credit card information to use MongoLab even if you select the free version. You should not be charged for a free plan, though.

In order to connect to the database server, there is a database connection URL (a.k.a. MongoLab URL/URI), which is a way to transfer all of the necessary information to make a connection to the database in one string.

The database connection string MONGOLAB_URI has the following format:

```
mongodb://user:pass@server_NAME.mongolab.com:PORT/db_name
```

You could either copy the MongoLab URL string from the Heroku web site (and hard-code it) or get the string from the Node.js process.env object:

```
process.env.MONGOLAB_URI
```

or

```
const connectionUri = url.parse(process.env.MONGOLAB_URI)
```

The global object process gives access to environment variables via process.env. Heroku and Heroku add-ons like mLabs use these environment variables to pass database host names and ports, passwords, API keys, port numbers, and other system information that shouldn't be hard-coded into the main logic.

To make our code work both locally and on Heroku, we can use the logical OR operator || and assign a local host and port if environment variables are undefined:

```
const port = process.env.PORT || 1337
const dbConnUrl = process.env.MONGOLAB_URI ||
  'mongodb://127.0.0.1:27017/test'
```

Here is our updated cross-environment-ready `app.js` file (`http://bit.ly/2LeezQT`). I added a method to get the list of collections `listCollections` instead of getting the list of the databases (we have only one database in MongoLab right now):

```
const util = require('util')
const url = require('url')
const client = require ('mongodb').MongoClient

const dbConnUrl = process.env.MONGOLAB_URI ||
  'mongodb://127.0.0.1:27017/test'

console.log('db server: ', dbConnUrl)

client.connect(dbConnUrl, {}, (error, db) => {
  console.log('error: ', error)
  db.listCollections().toArray((err, collections) => {
    console.log('error: ', error)
    console.log('collections: ', collections)
    db.close()
  })
})
```

Following the modification of `app.js` by addition of `MONGOLAB_URI`, we can now initialize the Git repository, create a Heroku app, add the MongoLab add-on to it, and deploy the app with Git.

Utilize the same steps as in the previous examples to create a new Git repository:

```
$ git init
$ git add .
$ git commit -am 'initial commit'
```

Create the Cedar Stack Heroku app:

```
$ heroku create
```

If everything went well you should be able to see a message that tells you the new Heroku app name (and URL) along with a message that the Heroku remote destination was added. Having remote in your local Git project is crucial because that's you'll deploy the app to Heroku. You can always check a list of remotes by executing this command from the root of our project:

```
$ git remote show
```

Add-ons work on a per app basis not on a per account basis. To install the free MongoLab on the existing Heroku app (), use:

```
$ heroku addons:create mongolab:sandbox
```

Or log on to Heroku (https://elements.heroku.com/addons/mongolab) with your Heroku credentials and choose MongoLab Free for that particular Heroku app, if you know the name of that app.

The project folder needs to have Procfile and package.json. You can copy them from code/07-db-connect-heroku or http://bit.ly/2LeezQT.

Now you can push your code to Heroku with:

```
$ git push heroku master
```

Enjoy seeing the logs that tell you that the deploy was successful. For additional logs and debugging, use this command:

```
$ heroku logs
```

The result will be something like this:

```
2019-12-01T12:34:51.438633+00:00 app[web.1]: db server:
mongodb://heroku_cxgh54g6:9d76gspc45v899i44sm6bn790c@
ds035617.mongolab.com:34457/heroku_cxgh54g6
2019-12-01T12:34:53.264530+00:00 app[web.1]: error: null
2019-12-01T12:34:53.236398+00:00 app[web.1]: error: null
```

```
2019-12-01T12:34:53.271775+00:00 app[web.1]: collections:
[ { name: 'system.indexes', options: {} },
2019-12-01T12:34:53.271778+00:00 app[web.1]: { name:
'test', options: { autoIndexId: true }
} ]
```

So far you have implemented a local `app.js` file (`code/07-db-connect/app.js` or `http://bit.ly/2LhLrZm`). You enhanced it to work in the cloud (`code/07-db-connect-heroku/app.js` or `http://bit.ly/2LgX5Dy`). You learned how to build Node.js programs which work with MongoDB. Great work!

Let's enhance the latest `app.js` file by adding an HTTP server. After you get the `app.js` and the modified `app.js` files working, you modify the `app.js` to add a server so that the "connected" message will be displayed in the browser instead of the terminal window. To do so, we'll wrap the server object instantiation in a database connection callback. The final implementation is in the file `code/07-db-server/app.js` or at the book's GitHub repository: `http://bit.ly/2LcTd6K`.

Supplemental video which walks you through the implementation and demonstrates the project: `http://bit.ly/1Qnrmwr`.

```
const util = require('util')
const url = require('url')
const http = require('http')
const mongodb = require ('mongodb')
const client = require ('mongodb').MongoClient

const port = process.env.PORT || 1337
const dbConnUrl = process.env.MONGOLAB_URI ||
'mongodb://@127.0.0.1:27017/test'
```

```
client.connect(dbConnUrl, {}, function(error, db) {
    console.log('error: ', error)
    db.listCollections().toArray(function(error,
    collections) {
    console.log('error: ', error)
        console.log('collections: ', collections)
        const server = http.createServer(function
        (request, response) { // Creates server
          response.writeHead(200, {'Content-Type': 'text/
          plain'}) // Sets the right header and status code
          response.end(util.inspect(collections))
          // Outputs string with line end symbol
        })
        server.listen(port, function() {
          console.log('Server is running at %s:%s ',
          server.address().address, server.address().port)
          // Sets port and IP address of the server
        })
    db.close()
    })
})
```

After the deployment you should be able to open the URL provided by Heroku and see the list of collections. If it's a newly created app with an empty database, there would be no collections. You can create a collection using the MongoLab web interface in Heroku, then check in your app. You can use Mongo shell to connect to mLab too, e.g.,

```
mongo --username alice --password dolphin --host
mongodb0.herokuserverapp.com --port 28015
```

251

Message Board: MongoDB Version

We should have everything set up for writing the Node.js application that will work both locally and on Heroku. The source code is available in the folder `code/07-board-api-mongo` and at `http://bit.ly/2LbCtfX`. The structure of the application is as simple as:

```
/07-board-api-mongo
  web.js
  Procfile
  package.json
```

This is what `web.js` looks like; first we include our libraries:

```
const http = require('http')
const util = require('util')
const querystring = require('querystring')
const client = require('mongodb').MongoClient
```

Then put out a magic string to connect to MongoDB:

```
const uri = process.env.MONGOLAB_URI || 'mongodb:
//@127.0.0.1:27017/messages'
```

Note   The URI/URL format contains the optional database name in which our collection will be stored. Feel free to change it to something else: for example, `rpjs` or `test`.

We put all the logic inside of an open connection in the form of a callback function:

```
client.connect(uri, (error, db) => {
  if (error) return console.error(error)
```

We are getting the collection with the next statement:

```
const collection = db.collection('messages')
```

Now we can instantiate the server and set up logic to
process our endpoints/routes. We need to fetch the documents on GET
`/messages.json`:

```
const app = http.createServer((request, response) => {
    if (request.method === 'GET' && request.url ===
    '/messages.json') {
    collection.find().toArray((error,results) => {
      response.writeHead(200,{ 'Content-Type': 'text/
      plain'})
        console.dir(results)
        response.end(JSON.stringify(results))
    })
```

On the POST `/messages.json`, we insert the document:

```
    } else if (request.method === 'POST' && request.url ===
'/messages.json') {
      request.on('data', (data) => {
        collection.insert(querystring.parse(data.
        toString('utf-8')), {safe:true}, function (error,
        obj) {
          if (error) throw error
          response.end(JSON.stringify(obj))
        })
      })
    } else {
```

This will be shown in the event that the client request does not match any of the conditions above. This is a good reminder for us when we try to go to http://localhost:1337 instead of http://localhost:1337/messages.json and there are no messages:

```
    response.end('Supported endpoints: \n/messages.
    json\n/messages.json')
  }
})
const port = process.env.PORT || 1337
app.listen(port)
})
```

Note   We don't have to use additional words after the collection/entity name; that is, instead of `/messages.json` it's perfectly fine to have just `/messages` for all the HTTP methods such as GET, POST, PUT, and DELETE. The main reason why many developers and I use `.json` is to be explicit with the format that needs to be returned back. Another way to be explicit is to use `Accept` header set to `application/json`. If you change the endpoints to just `/messages` in your Node.js application code, make sure you update URLs in the provided CURL commands and the supplied Message Board front-end code.

To test via CURL terminal commands run:

```
[{"username":"BOB","message":"test","_id":"51edc
ad45862430000000001"}]
```

Or open your browser at the http://locahost:1337/messages.json location.

It should give you an empty array ([ ]), which is fine. Then POST a new message:

```
$ curl -d "username=BOB&message=test" http://
localhost:5000/messages.json
```

Now we must see a response containing an ObjectID of a newly created element, for example:

```
[{"username":"BOB","message":"test","_id":"51edc
ad45862430000000001"}]
```

Your `ObjectId` will be different.

If everything works as it should locally, try to deploy it to Heroku.

To test the application on Heroku, you could use the same CURL commands (`https://curl.haxx.se/docs/manpage.html`), substituting http://localhost or http://127.0.0.1 with your unique Heroku app's host/URL:

```
$ curl http://your-app-name.herokuapp.com/messages.json
$ curl -d "username=BOB&message=test" http://your-app-
name.herokuapp.com/messages.json
```

It's also nice to double check the database either via Mongo shell: `$ mongo` **terminal command and then** `use twitter-clone` **and** `db.messages.find()`; **or via Compass** (`http://bit.ly/2Lft3Qs`), **my tool** `mongoui` (`https://github.com/azat-co/mongoui`), `mongo-express` (`https://npmjs.org/mongo-express`) **or in case of MongoLab through its web interface accessible at the Heroku website.**

If you would like to use another domain name instead of `http://your-app-name.herokuapp.com`, you'll need to do two things:

1. Tell Heroku your domain name:

    ```
    $ heroku domains:add www.your-domain-name.com
    ```

2. Add the CNAME DNS record in your DNS manager to
    point to `http://your-app-name.herokuapp.com`.

Custom domains will hide the fact that your application is hosted
on Heroku. For more information on custom domains can be found at
`https://devcenter.heroku.com/articles/custom-domains`.

Tip   For more productive and efficient development we should
automate as much as possible; that is, use tests instead of CURL
commands Use HTTP libraries such as `axios`, `superagent` or
`request` to test your REST APIs. They are a timesaver for such tasks.
There is a chapter on the Mocha library and Node.js testing in my
other best-selling book *Practical Node.js, 2nd Edition* (Apress, 2018):
`http://bit.ly/2LdCNL3` and `https://github.com/azat-co/`
`practicalnode`.

Summary

In this chapter we covered the MongoDB database and its shell.
MongoDB uses an extended version of JSON, which is called BSON. Then
we switched to Node.js with the native MongoDB driver. Many other
MongoDB Node.js libraries depend on the native driver and build on top
of it. For this reason, it's good to know it. To use MongoDB on Heroku,
we utilized the MongoLab add-on (the magical `MONGOLAB_URI`). Finally,
we used the acquired knowledge to add database store (persistence) to the
Message Boards application.

CHAPTER 8

Putting Frontend and Backend Together

Debugging is twice as hard as writing the code in the first place. Therefore, if you write the code as cleverly as possible, you are, by definition, not smart enough to debug it.

—Brian W. Kernighan

In this chapter, we'll cover:

- Adding CORS for a different-domain deployment

- Message Board UI

- Message Board API

- Deployment to Heroku

- Same-domain deployment server

- Deployment to Amazon Web Services

© Azat Mardan 2018
A. Mardan, *Full Stack JavaScript*, https://doi.org/10.1007/978-1-4842-3718-2_8

Now, it's a good time to configure our front-end and back-end applications so they could work together. There are a few ways to do it:

- Different-domain deployment: deploy two separate apps (Heroku apps) for front-end and back-end apps. Developers need to be implement CORS or JSONP to mitigate cross-domain request issues.

- Same-domain deployment: deploy frontend and backend on the same webapp. Developers need to implement a static Node.js server to serve static assets for the front-end application. This approach is not recommended for serious production applications.

I cover both approaches in this in detail in this chapter starting with the recommended approach —different-domain deployment.

Adding CORS for Different-Domain Deployment

This is, so far, the best practice for the production environment. Back-end applications are usually deployed at the `http://app.` or `http://api.` subdomains.

One way to make a different domain deployment work is to overcome the same-domain limitation of AJAX technology with JSONP:

```
const request = $.ajax({
  url: url,
  dataType: 'jsonp',
  data: {...},
  jsonpCallback: 'fetchData,
  type: 'GET'
})
```

The other, and better, way to do it is to add the cross-origin resource sharing or CORS support on the server (`https://mzl.la/2LcH91Z`). It will require to add the OPTIONS method request handler and special headers to other request handlers to the Node.js server app before the output/response. This is a special header that needs to be added to all request handlers. The `origin` is the domain but can be open to anything with `*`:

```
...
response.writeHead(200,{
    'Access-Control-Allow-Origin': origin,
    'Content-Type': 'text/plain',
    'Content-Length': body.length
})
...
```

or `origin` value can be locked to only your front-end app location (recommended):

```
...
res.writeHead(200, {
    'Access-Control-Allow-Origin',
    'your-fe-app-domain-name',
    ...
})
...
```

We need a new response (route or request handler) with the OPTIONS method to tell the client (browser) what methods are supported on the server. The OPTIONS request can be implemented in the following manner:

```
  . . .
  if (request.method=="OPTIONS") {
    response.writeHead("204", "No Content", {
      "Access-Control-Allow-Origin": origin,
      "Access-Control-Allow-Methods":
        "GET, POST, PUT, DELETE, OPTIONS",
      "Access-Control-Allow-Headers": "content-type,
      accept",
      "Access-Control-Max-Age": 10, // In seconds
      "Content-Length": 0
    })
    response.end();
  }
  . . .
```

Message Board UI

Our front-end application used Parse.com as a replacement for a back-end application. Now we can switch to our own backend by replacing the endpoints along with making a few other painless changes. Let me walk you through them.

In the beginning of the `app.js` file, uncomment the first line for running locally, or replace the URL values with your Heroku or Microsoft Azure back-end application public URLs:

```
// const URL = 'http://localhost:1337/'
const URL ='http://your-app-name.herokuapp.com/'
```

Most of the code in `app.js` and the folder structure remained intact from the `code/05-board-backbone- parse-sdk` project (`http://bit.ly/2LfB9IQ`), with the exception of replacing Parse models and collections with original Backbone.js ones. So go ahead and type or copy the RequireJS block for loading of the dependencies (templates in this case):

```
require([
    'libs/text!header.html',
    'libs/text!home.html',
    'libs/text!footer.html'],
    function (
        headerTpl,
        homeTpl,
        footerTpl) {
```

The `ApplicationRouter`, `HeaderView`, and `FooterView` are the same as in the `code/05-board- backbone-parse-sdk` project so I won't list them here again.

We need to change the model and collection to this from using `Parse. Object` and `Parse.Collection`. Those are the places where Backbone. js looks up for REST API URLs corresponding to the specific collection and model:

```
Message = Backbone.Model.extend({
    url: URL + 'messages.json'
})
MessageBoard = Backbone.Collection.extend ({
    model: Message,
    url: URL + 'messages.json'
})
```

Next is the `HomeView` where most of the logic resides. I made a few enhancements to the rendering process, which is a good illustration of what you can do with events in Backbone. First, create the view and define the element selector, template (loaded via RequireJS and text plug-in), and event for the SEND button:

```
HomeView = Backbone.View.extend({
    el: '#content',
    template: homeTpl,
    events: {
        'click #send': 'saveMessage'
    },
```

Now, in the constructor of the view, set the `homeView` to `this` so we can use `this` later by the name inside of the callbacks/closures or use fat arrow functions `()=>{}` (otherwise, `this` can mutate inside of the callbacks/closures):

```
initialize: function() {
    const homeView = this
```

Next, I attach an event listener `refresh` that will do the rendering. Prior to that we had the `all` event, which wasn't very good, because it triggered re-rendering multiple times on the addition of each message. The reason is that `fetch()` triggers `add()` as many times as there are messages (10, 100, 1000, etc.). So if we use the `all` event listener for `render()`, our app will unnecessarily render multiple times. A better way is to use a custom event `refresh` that we will trigger manually and only in the appropriate places (you'll see them later). This will prevent multiple re-rendering.

The following code creates the collection, creates the `refresh` event and starts the `fetch` request to populate the messages from the backend:

```
homeView.collection = new MessageBoard()
homeView.collection.bind('refresh', homeView.render,
homeView)
homeView.collection.fetch({
```

The `fetch` method will perform a GET XHR request, and it has `success` and `error` callbacks (indentation removed):

```
success: function(collection, response, options){
    console.log('Fetched ', collection)
```

The next line will trigger rendering only after all the messages are in the collection (and came from the server response):

```
        collection.trigger('refresh')
    },
    error: function(){
        console.error('Error fetching messages')
    }
})
```

This event listener will be triggered by the "SEND" button as well as by the `fetch ()`. To avoid persisting existing records with `message.save()`, we add the check for the `message.attributes._id`. In other words, if this is an existing message and it comes from the server (`fetch`), then it will have `_id` and we stop the execution flow. Otherwise, we persist the message and trigger rendering on success:

```
        homeView.collection.on('add', function(message) {
            if (message.attributes._id) return false
            message.save(null, {
                success: function(message) {
                    homeView.collection.trigger('refresh')
                    console.log('Saved ', message)
                },
                error: function(message) {
                    console.log('error')
                }
            })
        })
    },
```

The rest of the `HomeView` object is the same as in the `05-board-parse-sdk` project. In the `saveMessage` we get the values of the username and the message text and add the new message object to the collection with `collection.add()`. This will call the event listener `add`, which we implemented in the `initialize`.

```
saveMessage: function () {
    const newMessageForm = $('#new-message')
    const username = newMessageForm.
    find('[name="username"]').val()
    const message = newMessageForm.
    find('[name="message"]').val()
    this.collection.add({
        'username': username,
        'message': message
    })
},
```

Last, we write or copy the `render` method that takes the template and the collection, then injects the resulting HTML into the element with ID content (`this.el`):

```
render: function () {
    console.log('Home view rendered')
    $(this.el).html(_.template(this.template)
    (this.collection))
}
})

app = new ApplicationRouter()
Backbone.history.start()
})
```

Here is the full source code of the `code/08-board-ui/app.js` file (`http://bit.ly/2LaHhCp`):

```js
const URL = 'http://localhost:1337/'
// const URL ='http://your-app-name.herokuapp.com/'

require([
    'libs/text!header.html',
    'libs/text!home.html',
    'libs/text!footer.html'],
    function (
        headerTpl,
        homeTpl,
        footerTpl) {

    const ApplicationRouter = Backbone.Router.extend({
        routes: {
            ' ': 'home',
            '*actions': 'home'
        },
        initialize: function() {
            this.headerView = new HeaderView()
            this.headerView.render()
            this.footerView = new FooterView()
            this.footerView.render()
        },
        home: function() {
            this.homeView = new HomeView()
            this.homeView.render()
        }
    })
```

```javascript
const HeaderView = Backbone.View.extend({
    el: '#header',
    templateFileName: 'header.html',
    template: headerTpl,
    initialize: function() {
    },
    render: function() {
        $(this.el).html(_.template(this.template))
    }
})

const FooterView = Backbone.View.extend({
    el: '#footer',
    template: footerTpl,
    render: function() {
        this.$el.html(_.template(this.template))
    }
})
const Message = Backbone.Model.extend({
    url: URL + 'messages.json'
})
const MessageBoard = Backbone.Collection.extend ({
    model: Message,
    url: URL + 'messages.json'
})

const HomeView = Backbone.View.extend({
    el: '#content',
    template: homeTpl,
    events: {
        'click #send': 'saveMessage'
    },
```

```javascript
initialize: function() {
    this.collection = new MessageBoard()
    this.collection.bind('all', this.render, this)
    this.collection.fetch()
    this.collection.on('add', function(message) {
        message.save(null, {
            success: function(message) {
                console.log('saved ' + message)
            },
            error: function(message) {
                console.log('error')
            }
        })
        console.log('saved' + message)
    })
},
saveMessage: function(){
    const newMessageForm=$('#new-message')
    const username=newMessageForm.
    find('[name="username"]').val()
    const message=newMessageForm.
    find('[name="message"]').val()
    this.collection.add({
        'username': username,
        'message': message
        })
},
render: function() {
    console.log(this.collection)
```

```
            $(this.el).html(_.template(this.template,
            this.collection))
        }
    })

    window.app = new ApplicationRouter()
    Backbone.history.start()
})
```

This is it. For your reference, the front-end app source code is in the `code/08-board-ui` folder and on GitHub at `http://bit.ly/2LfD1Bo`. I won't list it here because we had only a few changes comparing with the Parse SDK project. The next piece of the puzzle is the backend.

Message Board API

The back-end Node.js application source code is in `code/08-board-api` and at `http://bit.ly/2LbVY84`, which has this structure:

```
/08-board-api
    -web.js
    -Procfile
    -package.json
```

The `Procfile` file is for the Heroku deployment, and the `package.json` file is for project metadata as well as for Hekoru deployment.

The `web.js` file is very similar to the `08-board-api`, but has CORS headers and OPTIONS request handler code. The file starts with importation of dependencies:

```
const http = require('http')
const util = require('util')
const querystring = require('querystring')
const client = require('mongodb').MongoClient
```

Then we set the MongoDB connection string:

```
const uri = process.env.MONGOLAB_URI ||
'mongodb://@127.0.0.1:27017/messages'
//MONGOLAB_URI=mongodb://user:pass@server.mongohq.
com:port/db_name
```

We connect to the database using the string and `client.connect` method. It's important to handle the error and finish the execution flow with `return` if there's an error:

```
client.connect(uri, function(error, db) {
  if (error) return console.error(error)
```

After we are sure that there were no errors (otherwise the execution flow won't come to the next line), we select the collection, which is `messages` in this case:

```
  const collection = db.collection('messages')
```

The server code follows. We create the server instance and set up the `origin` variable based on the information from the request. This value will be in the `Access-Control-Allow-Origin` header. The idea is that the response will have the value of the client's URL:

```
  const app = http.createServer(function (request,
  response) {
    const origin = (request.headers.origin || '*')
```

Check the HTTP method value in `request.method`. If it's OPTIONS, which we must implement for CORS, we start writing headers to the `response` object:

```
if (request.method == 'OPTIONS') {
  response.writeHead('204', 'No Content', {
    'Access-Control-Allow-Origin': origin,
```

The next header will tell what methods are supported:

```
    'Access-Control-Allow-Methods':
     'GET, POST, PUT, DELETE, OPTIONS',
    'Access-Control-Allow-Headers': 'content-type,
    accept',
    'Access-Control-Max-Age': 10, // In seconds
    'Content-Length': 0
  })
  response.end()
```

We are done with OPTIONS, but we still need to implement GET and POST:

```
} else if (request.method === 'GET' && request.url ===
'/messages.json') {
  collection.find().toArray(function(error, results) {
    if (error) return console.error(error)
    const body = JSON.stringify(results)
```

We need to add a few headers to the response of the GET:

```
response.writeHead(200, {
  'Access-Control-Allow-Origin': origin,
  'Content-Type': 'text/plain',
  'Content-Length': body.length
})
```

```
console.log('LIST OF OBJECTS: ')
console.dir(results)
response.end(body)
})
```

Last but not least, we process POST:

```
} else if (request.method === 'POST' &&
request.url === '/messages.json') {
  request.on('data', function(data) {
    console.log('RECEIVED DATA:')
    console.log(data.toString('utf-8'))
```

We need to parse data to get the object so later we can save it into the database. The next line often causes bugs because front-end apps send data in one format and the server parses another. Please make sure to use the same format on the browser and server:

```
collection.insert(JSON.parse(data.
toString('utf-8')),
{safe:true}, function(error, obj) {
  if (error) return console.error(error)
  console.log('OBJECT IS SAVED: ')
  console.log(JSON.stringify(obj))
  const body = JSON.stringify(obj)
```

We add the headers again. Maybe we should write a function and call it instead of writing the headers manually. Wait, Express.js is actually will do some of it for us, but that's a topic for another book (read my book *Pro Express.js* at http://amzn.to/1D6qiqk). The following code supplies the CORS headers for the response:

```
response.writeHead(200,{
  'Access-Control-Allow-Origin': origin,
  'Content-Type': 'text/plain',
```

```
            'Content-Length': body.length
          })
          response.end(body)
        })
      })
    }
  })
  const port = process.env.PORT || 1337
  app.listen(port)
})
```

Here is the source code of `web.js`, our Node.js application implemented with CORS headers:

```
const http = require('http')
const util = require('util')
const querystring = require('querystring')
const client = require('mongodb').MongoClient

const uri = process.env.MONGOLAB_URI ||
'mongodb://@127.0.0.1:27017/messages'
//MONGOLAB_URI = mongodb://user:pass@server.mongohq.
com:port/db_name

client.connect(uri, function(error, db) {
  if (error) return console.error(error)
  const collection = db.collection('messages')
  const app = http.createServer(function (request,
  response) {
    const origin = (request.headers.origin || '*')
    if (request.method == 'OPTIONS') {
      response.writeHead('204', 'No Content', {
        'Access-Control-Allow-Origin': origin,
        'Access-Control-Allow-Methods':
```

```javascript
      'GET, POST, PUT, DELETE, OPTIONS',
    'Access-Control-Allow-Headers': 'content-type,
    accept',
    'Access-Control-Max-Age': 10, // Seconds.
    'Content-Length': 0
  })
  response.end()
} else if (request.method === 'GET' &&
request.url === '/messages.json') {
  collection.find().toArray(function(error,results) {
    if (error) return console.error(error)
    const body = JSON.stringify(results)
    response.writeHead(200,{
      'Access-Control-Allow-Origin': origin,
      'Content-Type': 'text/plain',
      'Content-Length': body.length
    })
    console.log('LIST OF OBJECTS: ')
    console.dir(results)
    response.end(body)
  })
} else if (request.method === 'POST' &&
request.url === '/messages.json') {
  request.on('data', function(data) {
    console.log('RECEIVED DATA:')
    console.log(data.toString('utf-8'))
    collection.insert(JSON.parse(data.
    toString('utf-8')),
    {safe:true}, function(error, obj) {
      if (error) return console.error(error)
      console.log('OBJECT IS SAVED: ')
      console.log(JSON.stringify(obj))
```

```
      const body = JSON.stringify(obj)
      response.writeHead(200, {
        'Access-Control-Allow-Origin': origin,
        'Content-Type': 'text/plain',
        'Content-Length': body.length
      })
      response.end(body)
    })
  })
    }
  })
  const port = process.env.PORT || 1337
  app.listen(port)
})
```

Deployment to Heroku

For your convenience, I placed the front-end app in `code/08-board-ui` and at `http://bit.ly/2LfD1Bo`. I also saved the the back-end app with CORS in the `code/08-board-api` folder, and uploaded to `http://bit.ly/2LbVY84`.

By now, you probably know what to do, but as a reference, below are the steps to deploy these examples to Heroku. We'll start with the API. In the `08-board-api` folder, execute the following code (`$ heroku login` is optional):

```
$ git init
$ git add .
$ git commit -am "first commit"
$ heroku login
$ heroku create
$ heroku addons:create mongolab:sandbox
$ git push heroku master
```

Watch the terminal messages. If the API is successfully deployed, you can test it with CURL or Postman. Then copy the URL from Heroku (e.g., `https://guarded-waters-1780.herokuapp.com`) and paste it into the `code/08-board-ui/app.js` file, assigning the value to the URL variable. Then, in the `code/08-board-ui` folder, execute:

```
$ git init
$ git add .
$ git commit -am "first commit"
$ heroku create
$ git push heroku master
$ heroku open
```

That's it. By now you should be able to see Message Board running in the cloud with the UI (front-end browser app) on one domain and the API (backend) on another. In high-trafficked apps, the API will be hiding behind a load balancer, so you can have multiple API servers on a single IP/URL. This way they'll handle more traffic and the system will become more resilient. You can take out, restart, or deploy on APIs one at a time with zero downtime.

Same-Domain Deployment Server

The same-domain deployment is *not recommended* for serious production applications, because static assets are better served with web servers like Nginx (not Node.js I/O engine), and separating APIs makes for less complicated testing, increased robustness, and quicker troubleshooting/ monitoring. However, the same app/domain approach could be used for staging, testing, development environments, and/or tiny apps.

The idea is that the API serves static files for the browser app as well, not just handling dynamic requests to its routes. So you can copy the code/08-board-api **code into a new folder** code/08-board-web **(or getting my copy from GitHub). The beginning of the new server file is the same; we have GET and POST logic (this time CORS is not needed). The last condition in the chain of** if/else **needs to process the static files. Here's how we can do a new response/request handler for static assets:**

```
const http = require('http'),
  url = require('url'),
  path = require('path'),
  fs = require('fs'),
  port = process.env.PORT || 1337,
  staticFolder = 'public',
  client = require('mongodb').MongoClient

const uri = process.env.MONGOLAB_URI ||
'mongodb://@127.0.0.1:27017/messages'
//MONGOLAB_URI=mongodb://user:pass@server.mongohq.
com:port/db_name

client.connect(uri, function(error, db) {
  if (error) return console.error(error)
  const collection = db.collection('messages')

  http.createServer(function(request, response) {
    const origin = (request.headers.origin || '*')
    if (request.method == 'OPTIONS') {
      // ...
    } else if (request.method === 'GET' &&
    request.url === '/messages.json') {
      // ...
    } else if (request.method === 'POST' &&
    request.url === '/messages.json') {
      // ...
    } else {
```

```
const uri = url.parse(request.url).pathname
console.log('Processing URI: ', uri)
if (uri == '' || uri == '/') uri = 'index.html'
filename = path.join(__dirname, staticFolder, uri)
console.log('Processing file: ', filename)
try {
  stats = fs.statSync(filename)
} catch (error) {
  if (error) {
    console.error(error)
    response.writeHead(404, {
      'Content-Type': 'text/plain'})
    response.write('404 Not Found\n')
    return response.end()
  }
}
if(!stats.isFile()) {
  response.writeHead(404, {
    'Content-Type': 'text/plain'})
  response.write('404 Not Found\n')
  return response.end()
} else {
  const file = fs.readFileSync(filename)
  if (!file) {
    response.writeHead(500,
      {'Content-Type': 'text/plain'})
    response.write(err + '\n')
    return response.end()
  }
```

```
    const extname = path.extname(filename)
    const contentType = 'text/html'
    switch (extname) {
        case '.js':
            contentType = 'text/javascript'
            break
        case '.css':
            contentType = 'text/css'
            break
        case '.json':
            contentType = 'application/json'
            break
        case '.png':
            contentType = 'image/png'
            break
        case '.jpg':
        case '.jpeg':
            contentType = 'image/jpg'
            break
        case '.wav':
            contentType = 'audio/wav'
            break
    }
    response.writeHead(200, {
      'Content-Type': contentType,
      'Content-Length': file.length
    })
    response.end(file)
  }
}
}).listen(port)
```

```
console.log('Static file server running at\n '+
' => http://localhost:' + port + '/\nCTRL + C to
shutdown')

})
```

Let me take you through this implementation line-by-line. We use the url module (https://npmjs.org/url) to parse the path name from the URL. The path name is everything after the domain; for example, in http://webapplog.com/es6 the path name is /es6. This will be our folder and file names.

```
const uri = url.parse(request.url).pathname
```

It's good to have some logging to know that our system is working as it should:

```
console.log('Processing path: ', uri)
```

The next line deals with the root URI; that is, when you go to the website and the path is empty or a slash, you'll get index.html. In our app, let's follow the convention and serve the index.html file by default (if it exists):

```
if (uri == ' ' || uri == '/') uri = 'index.html'
```

The path.join() method will make this code cross-platform by creating a string with the proper slashes depending on the OS: that is, \ or / as separator. You can see the resulting path and file name in the logs:

```
filename = path.join(__dirname, staticFolder, uri)
console.log('Processing file: ', filename)
```

I always say never use synchronous functions in Node.js, unless you have to. This is such a case. Without the synch methods, we'll get racing conditions on our files, meaning some will load faster than the others and cause conflicts:

```
stats = fs.statSync(filename)
if (error) {
  console.error(error)
```

Obviously, if the file doesn't exist we want to send 404 Not Found:

```
response.writeHead(404, {
  'Content-Type': 'text/plain'})
response.write('404 Not Found\n')
return response.end()
}
```

Let's make sure the requested resource is the file. If it's not the file, you can implement adding index.html as we did for the root. I don't have this code here. Our front-end app only needs to include files so this code will serve the files!

```
if(!stats.isFile()) {
  response.writeHead(404, {
    'Content-Type': 'text/plain'})
  response.write('404 Not Found\n')
  return response.end()
} else {
```

Finally, we read the file. We use the synchronous function again for the reasons mentioned above.

```
const file = fs.readFileSync(filename)
if (!file) {
  response.writeHead(500, {'Content-Type':
  'text/plain'})
```

```
response.write(err + '\n')
return response.end()
}
```

I know that the JavaScript guru Douglas Crockford dislikes `switch`, but we'll use it here to determine the right content type for the response header. Most browsers will understand the content type okay if you omit the `Content-Type` header, but why not go the extra mile?

```
const extname = path.extname(filename)
const contentType = 'text/html'
switch (extname) {
    case '.js':
        contentType = 'text/javascript'
        break
    case '.css':
        contentType = 'text/css'
        break
    case '.json':
        contentType = 'application/json'
        break
    case '.png':
        contentType = 'image/png'
        break
    case '.jpg':
    case '.jpeg':
        contentType = 'image/jpg'
        break
    case '.wav':
        contentType = 'audio/wav'
        break
}
response.writeHead(200, {
  'Content-Type': contentType,
```

Another header that we send back with the response is `Content-Length`:

```
    'Content-Length': file.length
  })
  response.end(file)
 }
}
. . .
```

So this piece of code goes into the request handler of the server, which is inside of the database connect call. Just like the Russian Matreshka dolls. Confusing? Just refer to the full source code at `http://bit.ly/2LdCK20`.

Another, more elegant way is to use Node.js frameworks such as Connect or Express; because there is a special `static` middleware for JS and CSS assets. But those frameworks deserve a book on their own.

Now that you've mastered the basics of Node.js, MongoDB, Backbone. js, and Heroku, there's one bonus step to take: deployment to the cloud. Check out the cloud solution Amazon Web Services known as EC2 (Infrastructure as a Service category of cloud computing).

Deployment to Amazon Web Services

Cloud is eating the world of computing. You can say that cloud has taken the world of IT by storm. There are private and public clouds. AWS, probably the most popular choice among the public cloud options, offers Elastic Compute Cloud (EC2) in the infrastructure as a Service (IaaS) category of cloud solutions. The advantages of using an IaaS such as AWS EC2 over PaaS-like Heroku are as follows:

- It's more configurable (any services, packages, or operation systems).

- It's more controllable. There are no restrictions or limitations.

- It's cheaper to maintain. PaaS can quickly cost a fortune for high-performance resources.

In this tutorial, we'll be using the 64-bit Amazon Linux AMI (`http://aws.amazon.com/amazon-linux-ami`) with CentOS (`http://aws.amazon.com/amazon-linux-ami`).

Assuming you have your EC2 instance up and running, SSH into it and install all system updates with `yum`:

```
$ sudo yum update
```

You can try installing Node.js with `yum`. It should be available in the Extra Packages for Enterprise Linux repository (`https://fedoraproject.org/wiki/EPEL`):

```
$ sudo yum install nodejs npm --enablerepo=epel
```

This might take a while. Answer with y as the process goes. In the end, you should see something like this (your results may vary):

```
Installed: nodejs.i686 0:0.10.26-1.el6
npm.noarch 0:1.3.6-4.el6Dependency Installed:
...Dependency Updated:...Complete!
```

You probably know this, but just in case, to check installations, type the following:

```
$ node -V
$ npm -v
```

If the `yum` Node.js installation fails, see if you have EPEL (just see if the command below says `epel`):

```
$ yum repolist
```

If there's no `epel`, run:

```
$ rpm -Uvh http://download-i2.fedoraproject.org/pub/
epel/6/i386/epel-release-6-8.noarch.rpm
```

Then, try to install both Node.js and npm again with:

```
$ sudo yum install nodejs npm --enablerepo=epel
```

Alternatively, you can compile Node.js from the source. To do so, install the C++ compiler (again with `yum`):

```
$ sudo yum install gcc-c++ make
```

Same with openSSL:

```
$ sudo yum install openssl-devel
```

Then install Git with `yum`:

```
$ sudo yum install git
```

Finally, clone the Node.js repository straight from GitHub:

```
$ git clone git://github.com/joyent/node.git
```

And build Node.js:

```
$ cd node
$ git checkout v0.10.12
$ ./configure
$ make
$ sudo make install
```

Note   For a different version of Node.js, you can list all versions with `$ git tag -l` and check out the one you need.

To install npm, run:

```
$ git clone https://github.com/isaacs/npm.git
$ cd npm
$ sudo make install
```

Once you have Git and npm and Node.js, you are good to deploy your code (manually). Pull the code from the repository. You might need to provide credentials or upload your SSH keys to AWS. Then start the Node.js server with pm2 (https://npmjs.com/pm2 and https://pm2.io) or similar process manager. pm2 is good because it has a lot of features not only to keep the process running but also to scale it as show in Figure 8-1. pm2 also has load balancing.

To install pm2:

```
$ npm i -g pm2
```

To start your application:

```
$ pm2 start app.js
```

To list all running processes:

```
$ pm2 list
```

```
[joni] ~/keymetrics/PM2 $ pm2 list
```

App name	id	mode	pid	status	restart	uptime	memory	watching
API	0	cluster	26076	online	0	2m	22.582 MB	disabled
API	1	cluster	26085	online	0	2m	22.527 MB	disabled
API	2	cluster	26274	online	1	2m	22.566 MB	disabled
API	3	cluster	26133	online	0	2m	22.563 MB	disabled
Worker	4	fork	0	stopped	0	0	0 B	enabled
Mailer	5	fork	26165	online	0	2m	15.125 MB	disabled
Front	7	fork	26865	online	0	12s	14.465 MB	enabled

Figure 8-1. *pm2 running multiple Node.js processes*

That's pretty much all you need to do. Ideally, you want to automate the deployment. Also, you might want to add some `d.init` or `upstart` scripts to launch your `pm2` or another process manager automatically.

Steps for other OSs on AWS are similar. You would use their package manager to install Node.js, Git, and npm, then get the code (Git or rsync) and launch it with the process manager. You don't need the process manager. You can launch with `node` itself, but it's better to use some process manager.

Now, while the Node.js app is running, executing $ `netstat -apn | grep 80`, the remote machine should show the process. For example, for a Node.js app listening on port 80:

```
tcp  0  0  0.0.0.0:80   0.0.0.0:*   LISTEN  1064/node
```

On the EC2 instance, either configure the firewall to redirect connections (e.g., port to Node.js 3000, but this is too advanced for our example) or disable the firewall (okay for our quick demonstration and development purposes):

```
$ service iptables save
$ service iptables stop
$ chkconfig iptables off
```

In the AWS console, find your EC2 instance and apply a proper rule to allow for inbound traffic; for example:

```
Protocol: TCPPort Range: 80Source: 0.0.0.0/0
```

And from your local machine, that is, your development computer, you can either use the public IP address or the public DNS (the Domain Name System) domain, which is found and copied from the AWS console under that instance's description. For example,

```
$ curl XXX.XXX.XXX.XXX -v
```

It's worth mentioning that AWS supports many other operating systems via its AWS Marketplace (`https://aws.amazon.com/marketplace`). Although AWS EC2 is a very popular and affordable choice, there are other alternatives as well: Google Cloud (`https://cloud.google.com`), Microsoft Azure (`https://azure.microsoft.com`), IBM Cloud (`https://www.ibm.com/cloud`), and others.

Summary

This chapter presented the descriptions of different deployment approaches, the final version of the Message Board application, and its deployment with two approaches: on different domains and on the same domains. We covered deployment using the Git and Heroku command-line interfaces to deploy to PaaS. And we worked through examples of installing and building a Node.js environment on AWS EC2 and running Node.js apps on AWS with CentOS.

CHAPTER 9

Conclusion

I hope you've enjoyed this book. I intended it to be small on theory but big on practice and to give you an overview of multiple technologies, frameworks, and techniques used in modern agile web development, such as the following:

- jQuery, JSON, and AJAX/XHR

- Bootstrap, CSS, and Less

- Backbone.js, AMD, and Require.js

- Node.js, REST API, and Parse

- MongoDB and BSON

- AWS, Heroku, and MongoLab

If you want to explore any of these topics in greater depth, check out the appendix, "Further Reading," for additional references (or do a Google search).

Practical aspects of this book included building multiple versions of the Message Board app:

- jQuery and Parse JavaScript REST API

- Backbone.js and Parse JavaScript SDK

- Backbone.js and Node.js

- Backbone.js and Node.js and MongoDB

© Azat Mardan 2018
A. Mardan, *Full Stack JavaScript*, https://doi.org/10.1007/978-1-4842-3718-2_9

The Message Board app has all the foundation of a typical web/mobile app: fetching data, displaying it, and submitting new data. Other examples include:

- jQuery and OpenWeatherMap REST API (Chapter 3)

- Parse Save JSON (Chapter 3)

- Node.js "Hello World" (Chapter 6)

- MongoDB "Print Collections" (Chapter 7)

- Backbone.js "Hello World" (Chapter 4)

- Backbone.js apple database application (Chapter 4)

Please submit a GitHub issue if you have any feedback, comments, or suggestions or have found typos, bugs, mistakes, or other errata: `https://github.com/azat-co/fullstack-javascript/issues`.

Other ways to connect are via @azatmardan (`https://twitter.com/azatmardan`), `https://webapplog.com`, and `http://azat.co`.

In case you enjoyed Node.js and want to find out more about building production web services with Express.js—a de facto standard for Node.js web apps—take a look at my other top-rated books *Pro Express.js, Practical Node.js 2nd Edition, and React Quickly.*

APPENDIX

Further Reading

You have reached the end of the book but your learning is just starting. This appendix provides a list of JavaScript blog posts, articles, e-books, books, and other resources to help you continue your exploration of full stack JavaScript.

Free JavaScript and Node Resources

- Node University Blog: `https://node.university/blog`

- ES6/ES2015 Cheatsheet: `https://gumroad.com/l/LDwVU/git-1CC81D40`

- MongoDB and Mongoose Cheatsheet: `https://gumroad.com/l/mongodb/git-874e6fb4`

- Express.js 4 Cheatsheet: `https://gumroad.com/l/NQiQ/git-874E6FB4`

- React Cheatsheet: `https://gumroad.com/l/IJRtw/git-FB2C5E22`

- JavaScript For Cats (an introduction for new programmers): `http://jsforcats.com`

- Superhero.js (a comprehensive collection of JS resources): `http://superherojs.com`

© Azat Mardan 2018
A. Mardan, *Full Stack JavaScript*, https://doi.org/10.1007/978-1-4842-3718-2

- MDN JavaScript Guide: `https://developer.mozilla.org/en-US/docs/Web/JavaScript/Guide`

- MDN JavaScript Reference: `https://developer.mozilla.org/en-US/docs/Web/JavaScript/Reference`

- Felix's Node.js Style Guide: `https://github.com/felixge/node-style-guide`

Good JavaScript Books

- *React Quickly: Painless web apps with React, JSX, Redux, and GraphQL* by Azat Mardan (Manning Publications, 2017)

- *JavaScript: The Good Parts* by Douglas Crockford (O'Reilly Media, 2008)

- *JavaScript: The Definitive Guide, Sixth Edition*, by David Flanagan (O'Reilly Media, 2011)

- *Secrets of the JavaScript Ninja, Second Edition*, by John Resig, Bear Bibeault, and Josip Maras (Manning Publications, 2016)

- *Pro JavaScript Techniques, Second Edition*, by John Resig, Russ Ferguson, and John Paxton (Apress, 2015)

- *Eloquent JavaScript, Third Edition*, by Marijn Haverbeke (No Starch Press, 2018)

Good Node.js Books

- *Pro Express.js* by Azat Mardan (Apress, 2014)

- *Practical Node.js, Second Edition,* by Azat Mardan (Apress, 2018)

- *Node.js in Action, Second Edition*, by Alex Young, Bradley Meck, and Mike Cantelon (Manning Publications, 2017)

- Express.js Deep API Reference, by Azat Mardan (Apress, 2014)

Interactive Online Classes and Courses

- Node University: `https://node.university`

- Introduction to NodeJS on edX: `https://www.edx.org/course/introduction-to-nodejs-0`

Startup Books and Blogs

- *Hackers & Painters* by Paul Graham (O'Reilly Media, 2010)

- *The Lean Startup* by Eric Ries (Currency, 2011)

- *The Startup Owner's Manual* by Steve Blank and Bob Dorf (K & S Ranch, 2012)

- *The Entrepreneur's Guide to Customer Development* by Brant Cooper and Patrick Vlaskovits (Cooper-Vlaskovits, 2010)

- Venture Hacks: `http://venturehacks.com`

- Webapplog (`https://webapplog.com`)

Index

A

Agile methodologies
    CD and integration, 29
    pair programming, 30
    scrum, 27
    test-driven development, 29
Agile web development, 289–290
Amazon Web Services (AWS), 282
Asynchronous JavaScript and
    XML (AJAX), 70

B

Backbone.js
    AMD. and Require.js, 168–179
    code base
        apple-home.view.js file, 162
        apples.js, 164
        appleView object, 161
        apple.view.js file, 163
        index.html file, 160, 166
        module definition, 167
        .template() method, 166
        types, 159
    collections
        fetch() method, 133
        homeView and
            appleView, 134–136
        index.html file, 138–140
        loadApple function, 134
        source code, 133
        where() method, 138
    definition, 128
    dependencies, 128
    development kit, 185
    event binding
        constructors, 142
        index.html file, 144–147
        loadApple function, 143
        model.set() function, 144
        on() function, 142
        render() function, 142
        setTimeout function, 144
        showSpinner() method, 142
        UX, 141
    framework, 127
    render() method, 132
    Require.js (see Require.js)
    views and subviews (see
        Underscore.js)
Back-end-as-a-service solutions
    (BaaS), 31
Back-end development
    cloud computing, 33
    HTTP request and response, 34
    MongoDB, 33

© Azat Mardan 2018
A. Mardan, *Full Stack JavaScript*, https://doi.org/10.1007/978-1-4842-3718-2

Printed in the United States
By Bookmasters